The Weasels

A Sensible Look at a Family of Predators

Also by Bil Gilbert
How Animals Communicate

The Weasels

A Sensible Look at a Family of Predators

by Bil Gilbert

illustrated by Betty Fraser

Pantheon Books

To Marjorie Gilbert for early help with this book

Contents

The Weasels

A Sensible Look at a Family of Predators

Introduction

A good part of my life has been spent searching out, watching, caring for, thinking about, North American birds and mammals. My interest and affection have been caught by a great variety of animals. However, when I am honest enough to admit it, I have always had an underlying preference for the hunting birds and mammals—the predators.

The special, obvious characteristics of the predators which enable them to hunt—speed, strength, endurance—are ones that men have long admired and sought to develop in themselves. The best evidence that the hunting animals are widely regarded as romantic figures exists in man's most romantic symbols: our flags, insignia, coins, seals, crests. Invariably it is eagles, lions, wolves, tigers, and other wild hunters who decorate these devices because we have taken them to symbolize the brave, the swift, the free. This romanticism is not very accurate. (A trapped rat shows as much or as little bravery as a lion at bay. Courage is a notion, an ideal of man, not a characteristic of unidealistic predators.) However, in all honesty, I know romantic notions have influenced how I feel about the predators and how many other

3

naturalists, biologists, and animal behavior students feel about them.

If one were to study natural history only from the battle flags and national insignia of man, he might reach the conclusion that predators are the animals men cherish above all others. This would be understandable but false, since there is a great difference between how most men feel about a stylized eagle on a flag and a living eagle in the sky. To put it quite bluntly we have a high regard for predators as symbols and a very low regard for them as living creatures. No other group of animals has been so generally hated as the hunters, nor so persistently persecuted simply for being what they are. Thus men will hunt deer because it gives them pleasure or because the meat and hide of the deer are useful to them. Yet a man who kills a deer feels no hostility toward the deer just because it is a deer. With the predators it is otherwise. Men have carried on a long vendetta against them because they dislike what they are—predators. This may be another reason why a good many other naturalists and I have great interest in and compassion for the hunting animals. In a sense we are on their side; we root for them as one does the underdog in an athletic contest. Also, I think the predators bring out the missionary in many naturalists. The popular dislike and persecution of these animals is so often based on ignorance, superstition, and hypocrisy that naturalists are often moved to try to set the record straight regarding the habits of predators and the effects of predation.

In a general way the abiding dislike of many men for most predators is based on two notions. The first is that predators kill animals that men would like to kill themselves—domestic stock and wild game; that the predators are so sly, persistent, numer-

4

ous that they present unfair competition to man. Presumably, a man with an automobile, a dog, a gun, as well as his famous brain, is simply no match for, say, a fox when it comes to killing rabbits. Therefore, to have any chance at all of bagging his own game, the man must, whenever he can, first kill the fox to eliminate this competitor. Secondly, there is the feeling that predators are cruel, bloody bullies who take pleasure not only in killing but terrorizing, torturing more peaceful animals. Therefore the wild hunters deserve to be punished, in fact executed, on moral, ethical grounds, because they are *bad* animals.

In following chapters these two arguments will be discussed in detail. However, leaving explanation aside for the moment, it might be well to state in the beginning that every naturalist, biologist, or ecologist I know believes these two notions are absolute nonsense. Predation is a natural, *necessary* element in the complicated system of relationships by which life supports life. Without predation, life in this world would be far different from what it is today, perhaps nonexistent. Predation—a mountain lion hunting, killing a deer—is not a destructive but a constructive phenomenon. In the long run all species, even deer and human deer hunters, benefit from the activities of the lion.

As to the belief that predators are the criminal class of the animal kingdom, for the time being it is enough to say that such words as good, bad, right, wrong, wicked, cruel represent exclusively human ideas and if they describe any natural phenomenon it is only that of human behavior. They simply do not apply to other animals, who have neither the capacity nor reason to consider, much less obey or disobey, human moral codes. Unless one is prepared to argue that a robin eating a worm, a mouse nibbling a seed, a man chomping on a lamb chop are examples of wicked-

5

ness, it is impossible to maintain that a lion eating a deer is wicked. No animal is able to produce his own food as a plant does, therefore all animals must live by using other living things, plant and animal. To single out, disapprove of, punish one group of animals for living by the same system we all do is both moral and intellectual nonsense.

A good bit of man's confusion and misunderstanding about the hunting animals is a problem of definition. The word "predator," as commonly used both by naturalists and the public, is misleading, and in fact almost meaningless. The dictionary and for that matter biological definition of a predatory animal is one "living by preying on other animals," and preying is defined as "seizing another animal to be devoured."

According to this definition the robin who seizes and devours the earthworm is a predator, as is the Cooper's hawk that seizes and devours the robin. However, none of us use or understand the word in this way; and we do not consider the robin to be a predator. Commonly, traditionally, even legally (for we have many laws regarding hunting animals), we use the word predator to refer to large, zoologically unrelated groups of birds and mammals who hunt, kill, and devour other birds and mammals. This usage makes very little sense and it would be better if we picked up some word like "zilch" or "calkin" to designate such diverse creatures as sparrow hawks and weasels. However, predator is what we do use to describe the hunting birds and mammals and is what I shall use in this book. But I would like to make the point that each time I write the word it irritates me, since I am using a word to describe only one group of animals when it could logically be used to describe most members of the animal kingdom.

6

Finally, in explaining the fascination for the predators, there is for me, for many naturalists, I think, a very practical reason. I have found that despite their reputation for being secretive, aggressive, even dangerous, predators are in fact among the easiest of our native wild animals to observe and know. The wild hunters have fewer enemies, creatures they fear, than do the animals that are hunted. Therefore they are not quite so quick to fly and hide as are the prey species. Because they are hunters, most of the predators show more curiosity about strange phenomena they encounter, are more inclined to investigate than are the prey species. Courage has nothing to do with this. The prey species fly when they come on something new because until proven otherwise it may mean danger. The predators, on the other hand, will often wait to take a longer look, longer smell, longer listen, because they are hunters, and it is to the benefit of hunters to take note, follow up new signs in their territory. Thus there are many examples of predators of all sorts actually following men. Often this behavior is misinterpreted, offered as evidence that the predator has some evil design on the man. However, the truth usually is that even if the animal is a large one, a mountain lion, wolverine, wolf, he does not trail the man as quarry, but as a creature who may flush quarry for him, or more likely still, leave behind food scraps or carrion.

All of which is not to claim that the predators are without fear of man. Most of them have learned (or they have not survived) that man is a deadly, dangerous enemy. However, their fears are somewhat less deep-rooted than those of the prey species. Because they are more curious than timid, the hunters are quicker to learn that a particular man, or men in a particular situation, are not dangerous. This seems to hold true in both the wild (bears, for example, swarming around picnickers in many of our national parks) and in captivity. You can spend months painstakingly trying to win the trust of a warbler without much success, but in two weeks a captured wild hawk (a bird with which I have spent much time) can be taught to respond to a man's whistle, and to eat from his hand. A young fox, raccoon, bear, weasel, or mountain lion can be brought into the house, allowed to move freely, raised much as you would a puppy or kitten. On the other hand, a wild rabbit, mouse, or woodchuck will usually remain a fearful cowering captive no matter how considerately treated. As with any wild animal, it takes time and patience to become acquainted with the predators, but the task seems somewhat easier and more rewarding with the hunters.

Being very much pro-predator, I find it difficult to single out one species or family of the hunting animals as my favorite. I have spent more time with the birds of prey than any other group of predators and I find them the most exciting and dramatic of the hunters. The raccoons are perhaps the most intelligent, the quickest to learn. The dogs are also clever animals and in addition are the most sociable of the predators. Bears are entertaining, playful, and the cats have to be admired for their spirit, independence, and sheer beauty. However, for as long as I can remember, another family of predators, the weasels (mustelids), have particularly interested me. Perhaps because the weasels, more than any other single group, seem to me to illustrate what might be called the essential nature of the predator, the fundamental aspects of predation.

The weasels are almost exclusively carnivorous. They are persistent, perpetual hunters. Though not as numerous as some of the other predators, the weasel family is a varied one, having adapted itself to many different territories and environments. Therefore, weasels are found everywhere in North America and everywhere have an effect on the number and kinds of animals that inhabit the land. Finally, the relationship between man and weasel is typical of that between man and predator in general. The myths and misunderstandings regarding the behavior of these animals are numerous, often fantastic. Many people have an instinctive dislike, even dread, for the members of this family. Few have a good understanding of the natural, constructive role of the weasels in particular, the predators in general.

For these reasons it is hoped that the following chapters describing the weasel family may serve not only to introduce these varied and interesting hunters, but may also provide a better understanding of all predators and the phenomenon of predation. In my own case, long association with weasels has given me, in addition to a little knowledge of these animals, a great deal of pleasure. Perhaps this book will cause others to develop a similar feeling for these native hunters. If so, I believe all parties involved will benefit.

The Mustelidae Family

The name weasel, which properly belongs only to the three small-est members of a large clan of North American mammals, is often used, as it was in the introduction to this book, to designate the entire family. In much the same way, all diurnal birds of prey are often called hawks, though hawks are actually only one sub-division of a family that includes falcons, buteos, eagles, and others. This practice inevitably leads to confusion—logical, grammatical, biological. There is enough misunderstanding regarding this family without complicating matters further by describing both the big, bearish wolverine and the chipmunk-sized least weasel as "weasels." A more useful, if less familiar name for this family of hunters is Mustelidae, and this is what I shall now call the family that I have been referring to as the weasels.

Not only does this avoid confusion but also Mustelidae is a par-ticularly descriptive name, emphasizing one of the best known and most obvious characteristics of this family. Nearly all of these animals are, to put it as politely as possible, musty—able to pro-duce a musk (must) from well-developed anal glands. The musti-est of all is of course the skunk, whose scent glands have evolved into effective weapons of chemical defense. Most of the other members of the family have and use similar scent glands, though not so spectacularly as the skunk. For example, one of the few disadvantages of keeping a ferret (a European weasel sometimes known as a polecat) is that when it grows excited or alarmed it reacts defensively by secreting musk in sufficient quantity and of a quality that leaves no doubt that it has been disturbed. In the same way it is a fairly easy thing to tell if a hole is or has been recently occupied by a weasel, mink, or badger. All you need do is to get down and sniff. One of the many names for the wolverine is "skunk bear," since this animal, next to the skunk itself, is perhaps the most formidable scent-producer of the family.

The purpose served by the scent glands is, in the case of the skunk, fairly obvious. The evil-smelling burning musk is a defensive device, one of the most effective to have evolved in any mammal. To a certain extent the scent glands of the other mustelids serve a similar purpose. While his scent-spraying apparatus makes the skunk almost invulnerable, the less spectacular muskiness of the other mustelids gives them limited protection. A fox, for example, may in a figurative sense hold his nose and prey on a mink if he is hungry and nothing else is available, but under normal circumstances he will try to find a more palatable meal.

The strong scent produced by the Mustelidae has functions other than defense. Many of the family have the habit of burying or caching carcasses, storing away food for future use. Either accidentally or intentionally they often mark these stores with their scent, thus making them unappetizing to other carnivores. Finally, the scent of the Mustelidae probably serves the same function as the urine of dogs and the glandular secretions of beavers: a method of chemical communication between animals of the same kind. The Mustelidae apparently leave scent signs to mark their territories, thereby warning trespassing members of their own species, and to attract mates.

Though scent-producing is a common characteristic, few families of mammals, certainly no other family of North American predators, is otherwise so various as the Mustelidae. All the dogs, cats, raccoons, for example, are generally similar in appearance and even in behavior. The Mustelidae are so dissimilar as to make it hard to remember that they are closely related. The big wolverine and the tiny least weasel; the desert-loving badger and the seagoing otter; the incredibly agile marten and the waddling skunk are as unalike animal cousins as you are likely to find.

In succeeding chapters devoted to the individual members of the Mustelidae, the special adaptations and differences between the species will be discussed. However, lumping all these apparently dissimilar animals together in one family is not simply a whim on the part of zoologists. Therefore, in the beginning it is sensible to consider some of the ways in which the Mustelidae are alike, their common family characteristics.

The Mustelidae are a very large, numerous family, not only in North America but throughout the world. In fact, members of the family are found everywhere but in Australia, Madagascar, and the Antarctic, there being about seventy species in all. The family probably originated in Asia and then, like the other carnivores, migrated to this continent some sixty million years ago. The Mustelidae, like all the carnivores, seem to have as a common evolutionary forebear a now extinct group of animals called the Creodonta. The creodonts were among the first mammals to appear in the Eocene and Oligocene era. At that time all the mammals, then a new type of animal, were in a sense unspecialized. They were smallish, the largest being smaller than a collie dog, and they all probably did some burrowing and occasionally ate some carrion. None were specially equipped as predators. However, the creodonts, apparently stocky, slow, clumsy little furred animals, had teeth that were a bit more adapted for crunching up carrion than those of the other primitive mammals. Given their slight preference for meat, given many, many accidents, given millions of years of evolution, the creodonts began to catch their own prey rather than depending solely on carrion. As this became more common, they began to specialize and in time the modern families of predators appeared, while the creodonts, unable to compete with the better equipped, newer models disappeared.

It is incorrect to try to show a direct line of descent from the creodonts to any one group of modern carnivores. The creodonts, it appears, were ancestors of them all, and most of our current predators began to specialize, go their own evolutionary way, at about the same time. However, when we consider the principal types of predators in the world today—bears, raccoons, dogs, Mustelidae, civets and cats—the bears and the raccoons are probably closest in appearance and habit to the primitive mammals. They are heavy-bodied and relatively slow-moving; they are the most omnivorous of the modern predators, vegetable matter making up almost as large a part of their diet as meat; and their teeth, the basic equipment of the carnivores, are less specialized than those of other hunters. The jaws and teeth of the bear and raccoon are made for grinding rather than slashing attack. The dogs appear to be next in line, being more specialized than the bears, and more carnivorous.

In the middle, in an evolutionary sense, of the modern carnivores come the Mustelidae. They have fewer teeth (38) than the bears or dogs (42), having lost one set of the grinding molars, and the teeth they have are more developed as slashing weapons. Though some of the family eat large amounts of carrion, they are as a group more fresh-meat eaters than the bears and raccoons. Last in line are the civets and cats, whose teeth are poorly adapted for grinding, being chiefly suited for shearing and slashing. As a result, they are almost completely carnivorous, devourers of newly killed prey.

When we speak of the evolutionary ancestry of living things we tend instinctively, emotionally, to equate the primitive with the inefficient, the dull, and stupid. This is a mistake. The bears, raccoons, and dogs, for example, are, as things are measured these days, probably the most intelligent of the carnivores, having a greater capacity to learn and remember than either the Mustelidae or cats. They are more primitive than the Mustelidae and cats only in the sense that they are closer in certain physical ways to the original mammal stock from which all the carnivores seem to have evolved.

In addition to jaws and teeth, the other obvious, conventional weapons and tools of the carnivorous mammals are their feet and claws. Here too the Mustelidae occupy a position midway between the bears and the cats. The claws of the Mustelidae are well developed in some species—such as the skunk, badger, wolverine— being exceptionally long and powerful. However, they are more similar to those of the bears, being blunt instruments for tearing, digging, pulling apart, rather than deft, slashing weapons of attack such as those of the cats. The Mustelidae all have five claws (digits) per foot (as do the bears—cats have five on the front feet, four on the back). Another feature that illustrates the position of the Mustelidae among the carnivores is their manner of walking,

14

the way in which they place their feet. An animal that walks "flat-footed," that is with the whole foot placed on the ground, is said to have a plantigrade gait. An animal that moves on its toes is a digitigrade. Bears and raccoons are plantigrades, as is man. The dogs and the cats, on the other hand, are digitigrade mammals, only occasionally placing the whole pad on the ground. In this respect the Mustelidae are somewhat mixed, being described technically as sub-plantigrade to digitigrade. The skunk and wolverine are flat-footed like the bears and raccoons, while the slim-bodied members of the family more frequently move on their tiptoes like the cats and dogs.

There is also a family resemblance in how the Mustelidae hunt. Generally speaking, their least important hunting sense is sight, most of them apparently being, in human terms, nearsighted. Their hearing is good but not exceptional, probably not as good as that of the cats and dogs, much inferior to that of the owls, who are the premier sound-hunters. However, their sense of smell is very keen, and in this area they are second only to the dogs. Some of the closest looks I have had at weasels in the wild have been when, by accident, I met them while they were trailing their quarry. Like dogs, when they pick up a fresh, promising scent, they tend to forget everything else. I once was sitting on a log in the Appalachians when a tiny least weasel came past, nose down, and ran directly between my foot and pack, oblivious to everything but the scent trail he was following (more than likely that of a chipmunk).

There is another characteristic of the Mustelidae which, since it does not involve an obvious sense or physical adaptation, is difficult to explain but is important in understanding the hunting habits of these animals. Through the years, observers of these predators have been impressed by what is often described as the restlessness, curiosity, and boundless energy of this family. These terms are somewhat unsatisfactory since we are attempting to describe animal actions by comparing them to human ones. (This is a common problem in trying to study and understand animal behavior in general. It is also probably a problem with no solution. We are human and can only understand and describe what we see in human terms.) A weasel that one sees scurrying about the underbrush, darting in and out of every nook and cranny, looks as if he is behaving like a restless, curious man. However, there is a great difference in the reason behind the apparently similar behavior. Perhaps the difference can best be explained in this way. The next time we see the man he may be sitting in a chair, may continue to sit there for hours on end, displaying little curiosity, exerting almost no energy. The weasel, on the other hand, if he is awake and well, will next be seen behaving just as he did before: moving quickly, restlessly, curiously about his territory. These are innate, inbred characteristics of the weasel and most of the other members of his family which he can no more change than he can the number of teeth in his jaw, nor turn off any more than he can turn off his appetite for meat.

Basically the reason for the weasel's notable restlessness is that he has a very high metabolic rate. This means that all his bodily functions, heartbeat, respiration, digestion, etc., are very rapid. In a sense he is powered by a living motor which runs at a very high speed and which he is incapable of gearing down to a lower speed. This means that the weasel, who is constantly on the go, needs, like any other high-speed motor, a lot of fuel (food) and must refuel— eat and kill—more frequently than a less active animal.

When compared to the slow methodical foraging of a bear, the cunning, almost strategic sense of a dog, the stealthy, stalking tactics of a cat, the hunting style of the weasel appears to be a hit or miss, accidental affair. Actually the restlessness of the weasel is in itself a very efficient hunting technique. These predators persistently scurry, lope, poke about their rather large territories, investigating everything until they see something, hear something, or, more often, pick up a scent that will lead them to prey. A bear, for example, will go to a stream either because he has learned or instinctively knows there are fish to be found there. A bobcat will lie in wait near a rabbit run. The weasel, however, just keeps moving, examining everything, until he comes on something useful.

With few exceptions all of the hunting mammals are quick, restless, energetic. However, in the Mustelidae these characteristics amount to a specialty and are so prominent that they often lead to misunderstanding about the nature of these mammals. For example, the slim-bodied weasels, the quickest, most restless of the mustelids, are traditionally regarded by many as being cruel, wasteful, "bloodthirsty" murderers. It is assumed that their hunting habits reflect an "evil nature" rather than their physical equipment and needs. Some of the myths and misunderstandings regarding the character of the Mustelidae will be discussed in chapters dealing with the individual members of the family.

While the Mustelidae are often regarded as animals of low character, the most important, long-standing relationship between these animals and man is not based on personality differences but on a physical characteristic of this family. Without exception, the pelts of the Mustelidae are used in the fur trade. There is a market for the fur of even the coarse-haired members of the family—skunk, badger, and wolverine—while the otter, mink, marten, fisher, weasel, whose coats are rich in color, dense and soft, have historically been the most valuable furbearers in North America. Two rodents—the beaver and muskrat—have, because they are numerous, probably supplied more pelts for the fur trade than any other animals, but the skins of the Mustelidae have always been the most valuable.

Currently, a trapper can sell a prime otter pelt for fifty dollars, that of a mink for fifteen dollars, a marten for seventy-five dollars. There have been many times in the past when the pelts of these animals have been more valuable. (The value fluctuates depending upon what is fashionable among makers of coats, jackets, neck pieces, hats.) However, since the time of the first Europeans, the skins of these animals have been sought. There have always been professional trappers and in fact, these men, seeking skins, were the first to explore much of this continent. Also there have always been thousands of essentially amateur trappers, farm boys, for example, who will set out a few traps on the creek in the back pasture, hoping for a mink or two during the winter, praying that they might just be lucky enough to get a marten or otter.

While concerned and pure-minded conservationists have for many years objected to the trapping of the Mustelidae and other furbearers, it is much easier to understand and excuse the trapper than the casual hunter or predator-hater who kills these animals for no better reason than satisfying his misguided sense of vengeance. I personally would rather see a mink alive, darting about a stream course, than dead, draped over a woman's neck, but that is a matter of taste, fashion, and style, none of which was created by the fur trapper. He is in a sense a predator, preying on the Mustelidae, but he is doing so for a reason. The trapper makes sense in the same way that mink preying on rabbits make sense.

Nevertheless, there is no disputing the fact that the centuries-long trapping of the Mustelidae has put pressure on these animals, affected their numbers, ranges, and, to a certain extent, habits. By and large, as might be expected, the effect has been to make them scarcer, less widely distributed than they once were. The otter, marten, fisher, and wolverine are now very rare within the continental United States, while badgers and weasels have become less common. This is partly because we have altered the original environment, making it less hospitable for these creatures (and many, many others) than it was before the European settlement. However, in addition to these environmental reasons, the chief direct cause in the decline of most of these animals has been that they have been persistently and effectively trapped.

Yet, to be fair about the matter, some recent developments in the fur industry have, for some species, had the effect of partly undoing the damage done by excessive trapping. A good example is the mink, the most common of the valuable furbearing Mustelidae. The mink has been a prize for trappers (as well as fur-coat wearers) for centuries. During the twentieth century the demand for mink increased as the supply of wild mink decreased. As a result, various men with a good knowledge of the fur trade began to experiment with raising mink in pens, on ranches. Currently, most of the pelts used by the fashion industry come from ranch-bred and -reared mink. It has been found that it is both easier and cheaper to raise the animals on a farm than to trap them in the wild. Furthermore, through selective, controlled breeding, new fur colors and qualities have been produced. So far as wild mink are concerned, all of this has been a development for the better. Trapping pressure on the wild population has been sharply reduced in the past two decades, and the mink has now re-established itself throughout most of its former range, and in many places is probably more common now than it has been for a century.

There are indications that several other of the mustelids may, because their fur is so valuable, benefit in the same way that the mink has. On a small scale, otters and martens are being raised in captivity now, and if it becomes economically desirable, experiments in this direction will probably be made with other members of the family.

The situation regarding the Mustelidae is at the moment a peculiar one. Because of their fur they are, and have been for many years, economically the most valuable of all the North American predators. Because they are valuable they have been pursued relentlessly by man with the effect that their numbers have been drastically reduced, reduced to the point of virtual extinction in some cases. However, it is just because they are valuable that many people have an obvious economic interest in seeing their numbers increase. All of which might be regarded as a lesson in economic ecology. At the moment, many of the mustelids are relatively rare animals. However, the long range prospects of these animals surviving as our world becomes more civilized, more man-dominated are, because they are economically desirable, perhaps better than those of some predators—the birds of prey, cats, dogs, bears—which are now more numerous.

North American Members of the Mustelidae Family

The Weasels: Three principal species of weasels (and numerous subspecies) are found in North America. They are the least weasel (*Mustela rixosa*), the shorttail weasel (*Mustela erminea*), and the longtail weasel (*Mustela frenata*). All three (and all of the slim-bodied members of the Mustelidae) are long, lithe, sometimes described as snakelike animals, almost neckless with sharp-pointed muzzles. The least weasel is the smallest, and also the smallest of all carnivorous mammals, the head and body measuring about six inches, the tail an inch and a half, and weighing less than two ounces. The shorttail and longtail weasels are somewhat larger, the body length being up to ten inches. All three are similarly marked, being in the summer dark—brownish-yellowish—above; light—white, white-yellowish—below. All three animals may turn white during the winter, particularly those living in the northern part of their range. The longtail weasel is found virtually everywhere within the continental United States. The other two weasels are found only in the northern tier of states (excepting the Great Plains) and north to the Arctic.

Mink (*Mustela vison*): The mink is found throughout the United States north to Alaska except in the arid regions of the southwest. Within their range the mink is usually found near water. The body length is twelve to eighteen inches, the tail five to nine inches, and the weight is about two pounds. The tail is bushy. The fur is rich, dark, almost chocolate brown with a white patch under the chin. Occasionally there are lighter markings on the underparts.

Black-footed Ferret (*Mustela nigripes*) : This is very likely the rarest mammal in North America and was for many years thought to be extinct. Found in the central Great Plains states and the foothills of the Rockies, it apparently lives in close association with prairie dogs, preying on these rodents, using their burrows. Because of its rarity, information is incomplete and probably inaccurate. It is about mink size. The overall color is a light-yellowish brown with a black-tipped tail, black feet and a prominent black facial mask.

Marten (*Martes americana*) : The marten is slightly larger than the mink, but with longer legs and a more upright appearance. The fur is yellowish brown, very soft and dense. It is an arboreal animal, hunting and spending most of its life in the trees. It is found in the western mountains, north to Alaska, across Canada and in the extreme northern areas of New England.

Fisher (*Martes pennanti*): A much larger version of the marten, found throughout the same territory. The head and body length of the fisher is approximately two feet, the tail twelve to sixteen inches. It may sometimes weigh twenty pounds, though ten- to twelve-pound animals are more common. The fur is dark brown, so dark as to appear black. Like the marten, it is a good (though not quite as good) climber, and like the mink, is often found near water.

River Otter (*Lutra canadensis*): This is another large mustelid, weighing up to twenty pounds. The body may be two and a half feet long, the tail a foot and a half. The otter is an aquatic animal with webbed feet, a long, flat, tapering tail. Like the mink, it is found everywhere except in the waterless southwest. However, it is not common in any part of its range.

23

Sea Otter (*Enhydra lutris*): The largest of the North American mustelids, the sea otter may be almost four feet long and weigh thirty to forty pounds. It is a totally aquatic and marine animal found only along the western seacoast from California to the Aleutian Islands. The feet are completely webbed, almost flipper-like, and its life style, even appearance, is seal-like. The color is similar to the river otter, but white-tipped guard hairs give it a grizzled look. It is everywhere very rare.

(The species listed above are all somewhat similar in appearance, being elongated, lithe, sinuous animals, and are often called the "slim-bodied" weasels. The three following species are much different in conformation, being stocky, heavy animals and therefore sometimes referred to as the "stout-bodied" weasels.)

Striped Skunk (*Mephitis mephitis*): The skunk is probably the most numerous member of the weasel family, being found from Mexico to Canada except in the extreme northwest corner of the continental United States. It has adapted well to man and everywhere within its range is fairly common. The skunk may weigh as much as twelve pounds, the body length is twelve to eighteen inches, and the plumelike tail eight to twelve inches. The familiar black and white coloration varies considerably from individual to individual, some being almost all black, some being predominantly white. The most frequent pattern is a broad white V-shaped stripe down the back from the forehead to tail. Three other species of skunks—the hooded (*mephitis macroura*), hognose (*Conepatus leuconotus*), and spotted (*Spilogale putorius*), are smaller animals, less common and less widely distributed. The spotted skunk is found across the southern half of the United States, north to the Middle Atlantic, upper Great Plains regions. The hognose and hooded skunks are found only in the southwestern portions of the country.

25

Badger (*Taxidea taxus*): The badger is a large, burrowing mustelid found everywhere west of the Mississippi and occasionally as far east as Michigan and Ohio, in areas where the digging is good. The badger is a flat, short-legged animal and may weigh as much as thirty pounds. The body is about two feet long and the short tail only six inches. The fur is coarse, grayish yellow. There is a narrow white stripe running from the nose to the middle of the back. The feet are black and there are patches of black on the muzzle and below the ears. The foreclaws are long, prominent, and strong.

Wolverine (*Gulo luscus*): The wolverine is a burly, bearlike animal, weighing up to thirty-five pounds, about three feet long with a short (six to ten inch) bushy tail. The wolverine is found across the world in the polar regions and once inhabited northern New England and the upper midwestern states. However, now, in the United States, it is found only in a few scattered areas of the Rocky Mountains and in Alaska. The general body color is dark brown with a lighter stripe running from the shoulders down each side to the base of the tail. The fur is long and coarse. The front claws are long.

The Weasels

Like so many others, my first encounter with a weasel was brief, exciting, and involved violence. One morning when I was so young that I could spend my days as I chose rather than in a schoolroom, I was playing near our chicken house. (All of this took place in southern Michigan, where I grew up.) Suddenly a great commotion, squawking, flapping, scuffling started in the coop. I stopped whatever I was doing and went inside to investigate. As I opened the door, a small, slim animal, looking somewhat like a furry snake with legs, leaped off the roost board and darted past me. I slammed the door and raced after the curious beast. I was close enough behind to see him shinny up a small sweet gum tree. The animal perched in the top of the gum, allowing me a good look at him since the tree was actually not much taller than a big bush. He was about the size of a red squirrel, his coat was brown, soft, silky-looking. He had a pointed muzzle, tiny sharp eyes, no apparent neck, shoulders, or hips, his tubelike body ending in a short excited tail. As we looked at each other he made little squeaking sounds of fright or anger, sometimes showing, as he snarled, a set of numerous and what appeared to be very sharp teeth.

Guessing that as soon as I left the quick little animal would too, I stayed where I was and yelled for reinforcements. Very shortly my mother came down from the house. She was followed by a repairman who had been working on our telephone. When they saw what was going on, the telephone man became almost as excited as I was.

"That's one of those ornery little weasels," he announced. "Stay where you are, don't let him come down, sonny. I'll take care of him." The man ran back toward the truck. I thought maybe he was going for a net or box so that we could catch the weasel and examine him at our leisure. However, the telephone man had different ideas and came back with a shotgun that for some reason he carried in his truck. He stood underneath the gum tree and from there blew the weasel into a number of small bloody bits. While I was trying to keep my breakfast down, the telephone man gave a short lecture on the nature of weasels, one that I have since heard many times from many people. "It's good you found that little devil. They're the meanest varmints God ever made. Another ten minutes in that hen house and there wouldn't have been a chicken left alive. They kill just for the fun of it. Just suck out a couple drops of blood and go on to the next. Those little snakes will jump anything, a dog, a cat, they won't even back off for a man. I've got no use for them."

When the telephone man described the shorttail weasel (which I later found out was what I chased up the tree and to his death) as bloodthirsty he was using a word often applied to these little mammals, not infrequently used to describe all of the Mustelidae family and, in fact, predators in general. The idea seems to be that these animals are sick murderers: wasteful, destructive, dangerous creatures. There is also an implication that the blood-

thirsty weasels are bloodthirsty by intention; that if they wanted to, were not so wicked-minded, they could reform and feed on spinach, bird seed and maybe an occasional mouse. This idea of bloodthirstiness influences many of our feelings about and reactions toward all the predators, and since it is generally believed that the little weasels are the worst of the lot, it seems reasonable to begin an account of the Mustelidae family by describing the smallest members of the family and considering this accusation of bloodthirstiness.

As was discussed briefly in the preceding chapter, a fundamental reason for weasels being exceptionally active, persistent hunters is that they have a very high metabolic rate. The metabolic rate of an animal refers to the sum total of his bodily functions. These functions include, among others, respiration, heartbeat, digestion and elimination, processes by which the body converts food into energy and uses energy. Two good indications of the rate at which the complex biological engine that powers living creatures operates are body temperature and pulse rate. In man the average body temperature is about 98.6 degrees and his pulse rate, on an average, between 70 and 80 beats a minute. We are cold, sluggish creatures in comparison with the little weasel whose body temperature is 104.8 degrees (least weasel) and whose heart beats 300 to 420 times a minute (shorttail weasel). Also by way of comparison, body temperature of the mountain lion is 100.8 and the pulse rate 40.

What these figures indicate is that the weasels produce and expend energy faster than any of the other predators, faster than most other animals (some of the small rodents and shrews have even faster metabolic rates than the weasels). In other words, weasels use up fuel (food—which is converted into energy) at a much faster rate than most mammals, a fact that is very obvious to anyone who has ever had to feed captive weasels. In my own case, I found that both least and longtail weasels I have kept would and apparently needed to eat between a half and three-quarters of their own weight in food each day. These animals were caged and therefore somewhat less active than they would have been in the wild. Presumably the daily rations of wild weasels would be even larger than those of caged animals. Again in comparison, if men or mountain lions fueled up as weasels do, they would require about one hundred pounds of food a day to stay active.

There is still another reason for the exceptional food requirements of the weasels. They are slim, lithe animals, very strong and muscular for their size. The weasel does not, in a sense cannot afford to, carry much fat. Fat is tissue used to conserve and store energy. Fat first acts as insulation, slowing down the loss of body heat and thus conserving body fuel. Secondly fat is a kind of food reserve. If times become hard, food scarce, an animal will convert the fat into food and energy. Having very little fat, little stored energy, the slim-bodied weasel must refuel (eat) often, much oftener than most predators.

All of which has a predictable effect on the habits of the weasels. Whereas a bear during hibernation may go a month or more without eating, a raccoon a week or so, a cat or dog several days, the little weasels spend nearly every waking minute hunting for food. Furthermore, though they sometimes eat carrion, they seem to prefer freshly killed food and therefore must kill often during the day.

Even understanding that the weasels have remarkable food requirements, dictated by their physiological functions, it may seem somewhat paradoxical that such small animals should have such a reputation as ferocious killers. Even if a six-ounce weasel eats his own weight in food daily, this is still a very small amount. The explanation again rests on the physical characteristics of these animals. They are strong, quick, restless animals. To use a word familiar in the affairs of man, the weasel is equipped for overkill. That is, a six-ounce weasel is sufficiently strong, aggressive, and well armed to catch and kill a three-pound (or larger) chicken or rabbit. Again by comparison, this is a feat roughly equivalent to a man running down and then, bare-handed, dispatching an elk or small moose.

Now the weasel, like all wild hunters, is not out to prove anything or to brag about trophy-sized quarry. He simply wants food, and if given a choice will take that which is easiest to kill, which as a rule means he prefers small quarry. The diet of the three small North American weasels consists principally of mice, shrews, moles, young ground-nesting birds, frogs, small snakes, insects and earthworms. When he catches one of these small creatures, the weasel makes a meal of it, without much more waste than that left by any other hunter.

However, as said above, the weasel can, and if conditions are right, will kill much larger animals. Having killed, for example, a chicken, the weasel will eat what he needs at the time. Given the small size of the hunter, the large size of his prey, this may seem to a man who finds the dead chicken a very wasteful killing. To make matters even worse for the weasel's reputation, having killed a relatively large animal, the weasel may only tear at the throat, feeding mainly on the fresh blood. There is reason for this too. Blood is a source of quick energy for the weasel, who is always in need of a fast charge for his high-speed biological engine.

Blood, of course, is an excellent food, favored by many carnivorous animals, including, in some places and under certain circumstances, men. However, we North American men are not customarily blood drinkers. Therefore there is a tendency to regard the weasel, who does drink blood, and sometimes blood only, as a disgusting, wasteful, evil creature. There is little logic behind this prejudice. If vultures and dogs, who, if given a chance, will almost totally consume a carcass, were the dominant species, they would probably regard men as wickedly wasteful feeders, leaving behind bones, hide, entrails, and many other edible parts.

There is still another reason for the bad reputation of the weasels. Overlooking his blood-drinking habits, a weasel might be excused if, after killing the chicken, he fed on it more according to the fashion of men and other larger carnivores, that is, when he became hungry again he would return, eat a bit of breast, drumstick, and wing, repeating the performance until he had used up most of the flesh. However, the weasel is neither equipped nor inclined for such feeding. As said before, the weasels are restless and are not strategic, methodical hunters as are dogs, cats, men. Having killed a chicken and satisfied his hunger, the active weasel may be a long way away the next time (only a few hours later) he needs food and kills again. Or he may still be around the hen house. If so, the notion that the previously killed carcass is still available does not occur to him; he probably does not even remember it is there. Quite sensibly, from his standpoint, he simply kills another chicken and takes a few more ounces of food from it.

Such habits do not endear a weasel to a man trying to raise chickens. A chicken farmer who has a weasel move in on his hen house is well advised and, it seems to me, perfectly justified in destroying the wild hunter. However, the point that should be remembered is that the chicken-killing weasel is not acting in an unnatural, wicked manner. He is simply behaving as he must to survive. He is no more bloodthirsty or wasteful than any other hunter. Furthermore, in all of this it should be remembered that chickens, rabbits, other large (in comparison to a weasel) creatures are not the regular prey of these hunters. They are exceptional items in a weasel's diet, but they are the ones that catch the attention of men.

Much the same situation is true with regard to all the predators. Occasionally they will prey on domestic stock of man and when they do, there is a good, practical reason to destroy them. However, the difficulty is that too often men do not stop at destroying the wild hunter who is causing the trouble, but decide that every predator, everywhere, should be destroyed. This, it seems to me, is a true example of wicked, wasteful, unnatural behavior. Most weasels (and most predators) live far removed from men, having learned that it is unsafe to be too close to them. They are not in direct competition with man. Often they feed on creatures, mice for example, that are in direct competition with us. There is no practical reason for destroying any predator except the occasional one who has become a nuisance.

Nine times out of ten, or perhaps, since no survey of such matters has ever been made, ninety-nine times out of a hundred, a weasel, as well as other predators, kills for the reasons described above, because they or their young need to eat. However, a different motive seems to be involved when, occasionally, a wild hunter will kill for what in human and, perhaps, animal terms can best be described as sport—chasing their quarry when they are not hungry and, having made the catch, dispatching it without feeding on it. This relatively rare behavior, often misunderstood by men, frequently causes irrational responses. Antipredator types, the kind who regard all wild hunters as wicked varmints, seem to believe that most predators spend most of their time killing for the sheer pleasure of it. The nature lover, particularly predator defenders, often deny that such behavior ever does occur, claiming that hunting animals only kill for food. Both views are false. Either to exaggerate the frequency with which predators engage in what might be called sport hunting, or to deny that they ever engage in it, is to ignore an interesting, instructive, and perfectly natural facet of predatory behavior.

Anyone who has kept a cat or dog may have witnessed sport-hunting incidents. A cat, for example, will catch and play with a mouse or young rabbit, maul the animal until it is dead, then leave it uneaten on a doorstep, or, as our cats often do, in a chair. Most dogs chase squirrels and usually fail to catch them. However, once in a great while the dog will get lucky, surprise a squirrel on the ground, kill it with a shake, paw it for a moment, then abandon the carcass. Similar incidents have been reported in the wild—bears, lions, wolves, coyotes, preying without feeding on sheep or cattle; mustelids and other small predators on barnyard fowl. Usually such incidents involve domestic stock, and thus catch the attention and arouse the anger of stockmen. The reason seems to be that only domestic animals, large herds or flocks of relatively inactive creatures, artificially penned, ordinarily offer wild hunters much chance to kill easily and at will.

Often what is called sport hunting involves young predatory animals, who, in a sense, are learning their trade. Thus this behavior has instructional value for the hunter. But adult animals will also sometimes kill without consuming. I think the reason is that the compulsion or instinct to hunt is immensely strong in all surviving species of predators—if it were not, they would not have survived. These instincts are easily, in fact, automatically, triggered by certain sensations, of which hunger is perhaps the strongest. The sight of a running squirrel, however, or the rustle of a mouse in the grass can also trigger the hunting instincts of a dog or cat. The alarm signs of prey—the milling, bleating, stampeding of sheep, the squawking, flapping of panicky hens—also touch off this compulsive pursuit behavior. Once the chase begins, the killing, if it eventually occurs, is only incidental, being the last act in the hunting drama, in which the role of the wild hunter is irrevocably fixed. I have always been struck when observing such incidents that if the hunter is successful in one of these sport chases and eventually kills his prey, he invariably shows signs of puzzlement. Not being hungry, the question of what to do with the dead squirrel or sheep baffles him, and understandably so, since he has chased simply to chase, not to secure a meal.

What might be called sport hunting occurs relatively infrequently, since predators have little leisure and not much facility for creating food surpluses and therefore usually need what they catch. Among most predators, sport hunting, like predation, never constitutes a serious, unnatural threat to prey species. The one exception is, of course, man, who has the leisure, resources and inclination to kill frequently for sport, for nonconsumptive reasons. Not a few animals are now extinct because of the depredations of human sport hunters. The wild hunters cannot control their hunting instincts. Men can. Therefore, anyone concerned with this problem should direct his attention toward improving the behavior of man, which is theoretically improvable, rather than condemning predators whose sport-hunting behavior is fixed and has a very minor impact on other creatures.

36

Despite their reputation for bloodthirstiness, weasels have not suffered man's wrath to the same extent that some of the larger, more conspicuous predators have. Their size, habits, and agility have given them a certain immunity from the prejudice and vengeance of man. Though there are a good many so-called sportsmen who gladly deal with a weasel as the telephone repairman did with the first one I ever saw, the opportunities for doing so are infrequent.

From the standpoint of man, the three little weasels of North America are secretive animals. Though, when necessary, they will hunt at any time of day, they tend to be nocturnal, most active in the dark, using their noses rather than their eyes to follow their prey. Also, most weasels live, breed, and hunt under cover—the tangled underbrush of the forest, overgrown fields, rock piles, the thickets of fence rows. In this environment they spend much of their time following the under-the-grass trails of mice, rabbit runs, and tunnels of other small rodents and insectivores. Though the weasels are not particularly equipped or inclined to dig their own burrows, they are so lithe and agile that they can follow the burrows of almost any other hole-digging mammal in North America.

Typically, home for a weasel family is an abandoned rabbit, woodchuck, or ground squirrel den, though occasionally they will use a hollow log or the trunk of a standing tree. Being secretive and to some extent subterranean animals, the family life of the weasels is not well documented. However, it is known that weasels mate in the summer, though gestation is delayed and the young are born in late March or April of the following spring. There may be as many as a dozen in a litter of young weasels, though seven or eight is probably a more common size. The young are blind for three weeks, weaned at five weeks. Then the young animals begin to learn to hunt for themselves, under the instruction (by example) of both parents, the male taking part in teaching his offspring their craft as well as hunting for the brood. Families of weasels probably stay together until midsummer, when the young begin to drift off or, if they linger too long, are driven off by their parents. The dispersal of animal families is an interesting and instructive phenomenon. Normally a pair of weasels have a hunting territory of two to three hundred acres. This area will support two adults and their young, but only for a relatively short time, through the summer months when the living is easy, when the species on which the weasels prey—mice and other rodents—are also raising their young. By fall, when the numbers of the prey species have been reduced—by predation, competition with their own kind, dwindling food supplies—the territory can no longer support two adults and seven or eight nearly mature animals. Therefore, the hunger of the young, the hunger of the adults who grow less and less generous in sharing their kills, forces the offspring to move off and establish their own territories.

Another factor tends to disperse or at least thin out a weasel family. Despite being strong, aggressive hunters, the weasels are very small and are themselves hunted by a number of larger predators. In fact, weasels have more natural enemies than any other member of the Mustelidae family. Large snakes probably account for a good many weasels, particularly litters of relatively helpless young. Birds of prey, foxes, coyotes, domestic dogs and cats, even the weasels' larger cousins, such as the badger, fisher, marten, all will prey on weasels.

In their own hunting, the weasels, as has been mentioned, depend more upon sheer energy and constant activity than upon guile or strategy. Naturalists who have kept them under close observation report that a pair of adult weasels occupied with feeding a litter of young may travel several miles a night, though only venturing a few hundred yards from the den. The animals simply crisscross their territory, picking up the scent, sometimes almost literally bumping into their quarry.

Throughout most of their range it has been found that white-footed mice and meadow voles make up somewhere between fifty and ninety percent of the diet of the weasels. However, when the opportunity occurs, when they must, weasels are quite capable of preying on larger animals—rabbits, hares, squirrels, pheasants. Most of the stories about the weasels' ferocity arise from their rare, but more observable (from the standpoint of man) attacks on "big game." However, despite these stories, the outcome is often in doubt when a weasel tackles a much larger animal. Though they are quick, weasels are not particularly swift. A rabbit, for example, would leave a weasel far behind in a straight-ahead footrace. The weasel, when hunting such quarry, depends upon persistence and agility. A weasel on a scent trail is among the most determined of hunters, seldom leaving it until he has either caught up with his victim or been distracted by more promising signs. Most rabbits and other larger animals killed by weasels are probably caught in close quarters—a burrow, den—or in thick cover, where the large prey cannot use his superior speed and the maneuverability of the sinuous weasel gives him an advantage. Even after catching up with an animal as large as a rabbit, the weasel still has his work cut out for him. Though an agile contortionist, and ounce for ounce one of the strongest animals in the world, the weasel after all does not have much weight, and when tackling a three- or four-pound rabbit he may be overmatched. Several naturalists who have observed such encounters have seen rabbits beat off weasels by

kicking with their strong hind legs and eventually making their escape. Several of the larger western ground squirrels, if pursued underground by a weasel, often defeat the little hunters in underground free-for-alls.

Sometimes when the weasel attacks larger creatures the results are fatal for the hunter. A California weasel is reported to have attempted to prey on a medium-sized king snake; both animals died in the ensuing struggle. The weasel bit through the base of the snake's skull, but the snake, before dying, inflicted a number of wounds on the little mammal which proved fatal.

Such encounters are probably rare but there is no denying that weasels often appear to be very rash in their choice of opponents.

I remember one occasion when I went to investigate a squealing sound coming from the rubble at the foot of an old stone wall. I found a half-grown cottontail writhing in his last struggle; fastened tenaciously to his neck was a weasel. I bent down to investigate and the weasel, instead of turning and fleeing, leaped at my hand, chattering with rage. There are many similar stories of these animals, in defending themselves or their kill, unhesitatingly attacking dogs, cats, foxes, men, creatures of really monstrous (in comparison to a weasel) size. Such incidents should not be misinterpreted, as they sometimes have been, and offered as proof that weasels make a habit of unprovoked attacks on men, that the little hunter by the old wall intended to add me to the rabbit in his bag for the day. It does illustrate that weasels are incredibly aggressive little mammals. Their behavior in this regard is instinctive, and thus to speak of them as fearless, courageous animals (as we might of men who behaved in a similar way) is somewhat misleading. However, the fact remains that I am more inclined to admire than despise a six-ounce bundle of self-confidence who stands ready to chase me away from *his* rabbit.

Weasels also have the reputation of being cruel killers. Why this should be so is something of a mystery. Normally all predators attempt to kill as quickly and efficiently as possible. Long-drawn-out struggles exhaust them, increase the chances of the prey escaping or inflicting injury on the hunter. This is particularly true of the weasels, who have such outsized appetites and such a strong need and inclination to turn prey into meals as quickly as possible. They are, if anything, less likely to play with or maul their victims before killing than are the larger hunters, such as dogs and cats. When they are dealing with their customary prey—mice, other small rodents, reptiles, insects—I suspect the prey survives only a

few seconds after the weasel catches it. As do many of the predators, the weasel usually seeks to dispatch his prey by biting through
the neck at the base of the skull or slashing at the throat.

There is another story, perhaps superstition, regarding the hunting habits of these animals that has added to their somewhat
sinister reputation. It is that the weasel hypnotizes his prey, that a
rabbit, for example, will be immobilized by the evil stare and
appearance of the hunter. Such incidents—a rabbit freezing,
sitting helplessly as a weasel approached and then killed him—are
frequently reported, sometimes by what seems to be objective observers. Personally, I have never seen any evidence of the hypnotic
powers of the weasels, and I suspect that the basis for such accounts
may be somewhat less exotic than has been reported. Many prey
species would never be caught by predators (and many predators
would therefore not survive) if they did not become confused,
almost crippled by panic. As an example, I must turn to another
kind of hunter. Where I now live in the central Appalachians, a
problem that concerns hunters and game wardens are half-wild,
originally domestic dogs who roam the mountains and kill a number of deer. I have watched dogs involved in this kind of hunting.
A pack of mixed mutts, none of whom would have any chance of
running down a deer in an open race, will pick up the trail and
follow it persistently. The longer they follow, the louder they
howl, the more panicky some deer become. The deer will begin
running in circles of ever decreasing circumference and sometimes, though he is a stronger animal and has run no farther than
his pursuers, will at the end simply stand stock still, paralyzed by
his own fear while the hunters attack.

Such behavior, and I have heard of it in connection with other
predators, other prey, seems to occur most frequently in the case of

an animal which is pursued persistently. The weasels, of course, are among the most tenacious of hunters on the trail, more so perhaps than even a pack of dogs. Therefore it is not hard for me to imagine that a rabbit, chased back and forth through a thicket, might in time act as a deer pursued by dogs and simply quit running because of fright. It is also understandable that such behavior might be misinterpreted—that an observer might explain the curious incident as being caused by the hypnotic power of the hunter rather than the panic of the hunted.

Another physical characteristic of the weasels which unquestionably aids them in their hunting—and also protects them when the tables are turned and they are the hunted—is that the color of their coat changes according to the season, giving them year-round camouflage. The rich brown coat of the weasel blends in nicely with the rocks, brush, leaves during the summer and early fall. However, the same coat would make these little hunters very conspicuous during the winter, when snow covers their range. Therefore the weasel, alone among the predators (perhaps because it is the smallest and must depend most on secretiveness and therefore needs some extra advantage), has the ability to change the color of its coat from brown to white and back to brown again the next summer. No one is entirely certain what triggers this change of coloration, why the brown hairs in a weasel's pelt begin to be replaced with white ones at a certain time each fall. Temperature, the length of daylight, other biological timing devices have been suggested. However, it is known that the mechanism does not always work, and works differently in different individuals. Some weasels fail to turn, or turn slowly, being found in mid-winter still wearing their brown coats, or mottled ones. In the same way, white weasels are sometimes observed in the summer time. Another curious fact is that while most weasels living in snow country will turn white, members of the same species inhabiting more southerly, snowless ranges will not turn.

Whatever the cause of this seasonal camouflage, the advantage in making the animal less conspicuous, both as predator and as prey for larger animals, is obvious. However, curiously enough, there is a situation in which the adaptation has not worked to the weasels' advantage. Another name for the white-coated winter weasel is ermine, and ermine has been prized for centuries for making the richest, most resplendent robes and fur pieces. (Some fifty thousand ermine skins—winter weasel pelts—are reported to have been used to make the robe of George VI of England when he was crowned in 1937.) Thus, though the camouflage protects him from his "natural" enemies, the white coat has made the ermine especially desirable to trappers.

While weasels are still taken by trappers, the price of an individual skin is not high, less than a dollar a skin. It is the number of pelts required for a garment that makes this fur so expensive, and the demand for ermine in the modern fur market is declining. Therefore, trapping pressure on the three weasels of North America is not as strong as it once was. However, the little animals do not seem to be common throughout much of their range. The chief reason for their scarcity seems to be that the kind of environment in which they thrive—brushy, woodsy, covered places —is being so rapidly altered as we develop, urbanize, macadamize the continent.

Despite these changes, it seems possible to me that with a little understanding the weasel might reasonably be expected to continue to inhabit much of its former range and might even increase in number. All of this came to my mind a few years back when a friend, living in the suburbs of Washington, D.C., called me with an "animal problem." This family had a small backyard decorated with, among other things, a rock garden and a rather elaborate bird feeder. To the enjoyment of all, birds came to the bird feeders and chipmunks lived in the rock garden. The problem was that several times during the month, glimpses had been caught of a swift, snaky, brown beast darting in and out of the rocks. Having studied several guide books, they had decided that a weasel had moved into the garden. The prospect alarmed my friends, for they, like so many others, had heard horror stories about these "vicious, bloodthirsty" little animals. They wanted to know first if it was possible that what they had seen was a weasel; second, what would the weasel do to the birds on their feeder and the chipmunks in the garden; and third, assuming the predator would do something wicked, what was the best, quickest way to get rid of it.

I said that it was quite possible that they did have a weasel and if not a weasel, probably a rat, in which case—considering what a rat can do to bird seed and birds themselves—they might do well to go out and buy a weasel. If it was a weasel, there was a good chance that he would eat some chipmunks, but chipmunks breed at a considerably faster rate than do weasels. It was unlikely, I thought, that a weasel would bother birds on a feeder, since the food tray was mounted on a high pole in an open place. Finally, as for getting rid of the maybe-weasel, I said that if it were mine I would be very pleased, since weasels are much rarer than chipmunks or cardinals and certainly no less interesting. I may have been successful in my pro-weasel arguments. At least, as far as I was told, no offensive action was taken against the animal and he or his descendants may still be living in that neighborhood.

This one incident is not intended to prove that weasels are establishing themselves in the suburbs. However, I think weasels might do this, if permitted, to the benefit of themselves and many of us. Weasels are adaptable creatures and I think might in time learn to hunt and find breeding places in relatively populous areas, if they were not set upon with traps, guns, poisons, as soon as they appeared. As I told my friends, I can think of several practical reasons why a few weasels would be a good thing to have in any community. The mammals that have proven to adapt most easily to civilization are small rodents, usually considered to be nuisances —mice, rats, moles. One reason that these little creatures do thrive in city and suburban environments is that their natural enemies, the predators, have been displaced or destroyed by man. Now certainly one weasel, or even a family of weasels, is not going to keep a neighborhood free of mice or moles, but they will do their bit if permitted to. As to the dangerous or undesirable side effects of having a weasel about the place, they are not many for the average family unless they happen to be in the chicken business, which not many suburbanites are. Occasionally a songbird, a chipmunk, a squirrel, even a strayed hamster might be taken, but this would be an exceptional, rather than regular thing.

The big reason, as I tried to explain to my friends, for permitting, even encouraging, such an animal as a weasel to share one's yard, is that they will give a glimpse of a side of the natural world which is vanishing for too many of us. Of all our native animals, the hunters personify the wild, the free, the untamed. There would have been obvious difficulties if a mountain lion, bear, or badger had moved into my friend's yard. Symbolic as these animals might be, most of us live in such a way these days that we cannot share the land with these bulky creatures. How-

46

ever, a six-ounce weasel is as much a wild hunter as any, and is under most circumstances perfectly harmless. I have nothing against chipmunks or cardinals; I enjoy them. But because they are rarer, because for me at least they much better symbolize what is wild, I would rather see a weasel.

Now all of this, as I have said, is very iffy. I have no good evidence that weasels are learning to adapt themselves to urban areas or even that they can, but I strongly suspect they might. I think it would be a satisfying and worthwhile project if just a few of the many who are spending so much time and effort catering to chipmunks and cardinals, turned some of their attention to ways and means of attracting an occasional weasel to their garden.

The Mink

One of the most memorable wildlife experiences I have ever had took place six years ago in a high, frozen swamp. It is memorable (I can close my eyes at this moment and re-create the scene) and will remain so because of the unexpectedness of the moment, its beauty—and because of mink. Two other naturalists and myself had gone in March to a place called Cranesville Swamp, a fifteen-hundred-acre bog which is located on top of a three-thousand-foot-high mountain in West Virginia. For many years Cranesville has been an attractive place for biologists of many varieties—botanists, ornithologists, mammalogists, students of freshwater fish and invertebrates. The reason for the interest is that the swamp is located in what is called a frost bowl—a mountaintop hollow so shaped that cold air flows into it and warmer air flows out. In consequence, the temperature at swamp level in Cranesville is appreciably lower than it is even a few miles away. Because of this, the biology of the swamp is curious. The bog looks like one that you might see five hundred miles or so farther north. Many of the plants and animals of the isolated little swamp are found no place else in the vicinity, in fact are not found commonly until you get to New England or the upper midwest. Thus, for biologists the frost bowl acts almost like a natural cage, enclosing a tiny, unique community of plants and animals.

One of the unusual mammals reported to be present in this West Virginia swamp is the northern water shrew. As the name indicates, the little animal, which looks much like a miniature (six-inch) otter, is found customarily in more northerly areas, from New England across the northern tier of states into Canada. Very rarely an occasional animal will be located in the central and southern Appalachians. In the 1940s one was trapped in Cranesville Swamp. Therefore the three of us, all of whom had become interested in the water shrew, made several trapping trips to Cranesville to see if we could find another specimen. (We never did, though later we did trap a water shrew in a highland bog in southern Pennsylvania.)

Most of our trips were made in the winter, since we found it easier to travel over the frozen, snow-drifted swamp on snowshoes than to try to force our way through the interlaced thickets, oozing mud in the summer. On this particular trip the weather was ideal for our purposes. There were several feet of snow on the ground, the thermometer hovered around the zero mark, which is just about the right temperature for lugging trap packs through rhododendron snarls. We set some three hundred mouse traps along several beaver dams and the tiny overflow streams from the ponds. We finished making the sets late in the afternoon, just before dark, and then left the swamp for the night.

The next morning we came back an hour or two after dawn. The Cranesville frost bowl is encircled by a rough gravel road which at one point is intersected by an outlet stream from the swamp proper. We parked our Jeep by this stream and then followed it toward the area we had trapped, the frozen water giving us, on snowshoes, an open path into the swamp. We were within a hundred yards or so of the main beaver pond where we had begun our trap line, when the first man in file held up his hand, silently ordering us to be quiet. Then he motioned us to join him, which we also did. When we were together he whispered "mink," and nodded toward an opening ahead.

That there were mink in Cranesville Swamp was no secret, their tracks were to be seen everywhere in the snow. But the chance of seeing one of the animals was something worth stopping for, since mink, like weasels, tend to be nocturnal, relatively secretive hunters. We stood silently for a few minutes and then we saw our first mink, apparently a female (among the Mustelidae the females are almost always smaller than the males). She came out of the stream through a hole in the ice and slithered into the open swamp glade. Within a few moments she was joined by another, then another and another, and finally to our absolute astonishment and great pleasure, by six other mink. The convention of little hunters was apparently using the opening as a playground. It was mating season for mink, and though we saw no mating activity, this undoubtedly had something to do with the scene we watched. The mink played tag across the snow, dove into snow tunnels, surfaced a few feet away, pirouetted in circles and generally gave the impression of a schoolyard full of children at recess time.

It was, as I have said, an extraordinary experience, the little brown animals gliding across the white snow that shimmered in the early sun. What made it most satisfying from our standpoint was that the nearsighted mink apparently had no notion that we were nearby (the wind was blowing toward us) watching them. Normally when you come upon wildlife, you come as an intruder,

your act of observing changes the behavior of the thing observed, but this was not the case at this moment in Cranesville Swamp. I have seldom had such a strong feeling that I was a part, and not a disruptive one, of a natural scene as I did there.

One thing I remember thinking at the time, and have recalled often since, is that I had never before had such a good chance to see and appreciate the beauty and grace of movement of the mink. All of the Mustelidae, even the stout-bodied skunks and wolverines, have a similar humpbacked family gait. When they are running hard to escape, which is how one usually sees them, they seem a little awkward, but the seven mink at play were anything but awkward. Being long, short-legged animals, like all the slim-bodied members of their family, you do not get the impression of legs working as you do with a dog, cat, deer. They seemed to flow over the ground, their bodies arching, conforming to the terrain as they glided across it. The thought occurred to me that the mink in the snow moved like quicksilver across a tabletop, ever so smoothly, effortlessly. As I say, it was a beautiful and memorable moment.

It ended, we were all glad, very quietly, undramatically. The mink never did discover us; after fifteen or twenty minutes they just moved on, back under the ice, back into their burrows under the marsh grass. We probably had found them just as they were having a final romp to end a night's hunting, just before they retired for the day. We went on in a sort of wondering mood. The fact that these mink or others had played all sorts of tricks with our shrew traps did not lessen our regard for them, or our sense of good fortune.

One thing that helped make the scene nearly perfect was that it would be difficult to find, or even imagine, a more typical mink habitat than the cold, frozen, tangled swamp in which we watched the animals at play. In many respects the mink is simply a large weasel. It is much the same shape, hunts in the same active, aggressive way. However, the most notable difference between these closely related animals is the mink's greater fondness for a wet, watery home terrain. Though they are found throughout North America, they are seldom found very far from streams, ponds, lakes, and are particularly common in swampy settings.

Unlike their largest relative the otter, whose feet are webbed, the mink has made no special adaptations to its semiaquatic style of life, except perhaps for the thick, heavy coat that permits it to hunt and play in ice-filled water without discomfort. Nevertheless, the mink is an excellent swimmer and probably spends nearly as much time in the water as out.

Mink dens (often muskrat burrows that have been abandoned or from which the mink has driven the original occupant) usually are found directly on or very near the water. However, mink will occasionally move farther inland and take over a woodchuck or rabbit den. Mink mate in the late winter and the four to ten young are born five to six weeks later. Like the weasel, both the male and female parents assist in rearing the litter, both bringing home meat to the den and supervising the early hunting forays of the youngsters. In some cases mink have been known to treat their offspring somewhat like a cat will her kittens, picking them up by the scruff of the neck, carrying them to new dens. Also the adults will sometimes ferry their kits across water by giving them a ride on their backs.

Mink are tireless travelers and, being larger, the territory of an adult pair is more sizable than that of a weasel, sometimes including an area of two or three square miles. Also, being considerably larger and consequently stronger than the weasel, adult mink have fewer natural enemies. Only the bobcat, lynx, coyote, fox, and larger birds of prey are both big enough and quick enough to catch and dispatch a full-grown mink. Of these enemies, the big owls and diurnal birds of prey may be the most dangerous, since the very strong musk secreted by the mink (almost as odoriferous as that of a skunk) seems to repel only mammalian predators. Young mink, being smaller, have the same enemies as their parents plus some additional ones. Given their aquatic habits, it is likely that a few young mink are taken every season by snapping turtles and large fish, such as pike.

When it comes to their own prey, the tastes of the mink are varied. Like the weasel, the bulk of their diet is probably made up of mice, shrews, voles, for which they hunt in the meadows along the water. However, they also consume many more aquatic and semiaquatic creatures than do the weasels—young birds, frogs, turtles, snakes, salamanders, fish, crustaceans. When it comes to larger prey, the mink, like the weasel, will sometimes feed on rabbits, young woodchucks, perhaps on beaver kits, quail, pheasant, grouse, some of the low-nesting water birds, such as ducks and herons. However, the principal, perhaps one might say, the traditional, big game of the mink is the muskrat.

The relationship between mink and muskrat is a very close one. They share virtually the same range and the same kind of watery, swampy habitat, and as has been said, the mink often uses the muskrats' tunnels for his own den. When it comes to food, young muskrats are killed by mink who will sometimes break into a muskrat den or lodge and destroy the whole litter. Mink also prey on full-grown animals. However, in such encounters the outcome is not at all certain. The muskrat is larger than the mink (nearly twice as large) and is, for a rodent, a very strong, pugnacious ani-mal equipped with a formidable set of teeth. When, as a boy, I trapped on Michigan marshes, my usual companion was a cocky airedale dog, a notable fighter who seemed to feel he was a match for anything in the world, except a muskrat. His fear of these animals was real and long-standing. As a puppy he had gone with my father and me to check traps. Coming on one that held a large, very much alive muskrat, the dog rushed up to worry the animal. The muskrat promptly sunk his teeth into the pup's muzzle. The dog bore the scars of this encounter on his nose, and seemingly in his mind, for the rest of his life.

As it happened, during the same trip to Cranesville where we saw the mink at play, we also found signs in the snow of a battle between a mink and a muskrat. The muskrat had apparently come up out of the water to nibble on the tender bark of some low-growing shrubs. In the weeds his tracks and those of a mink converged, then grew confused. Bits of hair, both mink and muskrat, were caught on briars, and here and there were a few drops of blood. However, the muskrat had apparently fought his way back to the water and probably escaped. Though both animals are good swimmers, the mink is much quicker on land. Therefore, the usual tactic of the muskrat is that used by the one in Cranesville—to get back to water. Once in the water, the bigger, heavier rodent probably has an advantage. Among other defensive maneuvers, muskrats have been known intentionally to muddy the water, to blind and confuse the mink. Also, observers who have watched such battles report that sometimes a muskrat will get a good hold on a mink and drag the hunter to the bottom, holding him underwater until he drowns.

One of America's best-known, and so far as I am concerned,

most competent naturalists was the late Dr. Paul Errington. Dr. Errington spent many years studying muskrats—and their relationship with mink—in the sloughs and potholes of the upper Midwest. Dr. Errington's observations and the close association of the two animals illustrate one of the fundamental principles of predation, a principle which too few people understand and which everyone who has any interest in predators and the workings of the natural system must understand. The principle is that, overall, predation is constructive. A mink preying on a muskrat benefits not only himself but, in the long run, muskrats as well.

This can be at first a difficult idea to accept. After all, when a mink succeeds in killing a muskrat the profit seems to go exclusively to the mink. It seems this way because we tend to think of such relationships in terms of individuals. If there were only one mink and one muskrat, or even just a few of each species, then the destruction of a muskrat by a mink would not benefit the prey species. However, this is not the case. There are many mink and many more muskrats. The constructive value of predation only becomes apparent when we consider large groups of these animals —the species, not just one or several members of the species.

In his beautiful and informative book *Of Men and Marshes,* Dr. Errington writes of the winter confrontation between mink and muskrat populations in and around the frozen prairie ponds. The two animals are in contact with each other throughout the year, but it is in the winter, the hard time, that their relationship is most direct, most critical. In the summer, as Dr. Errington observes, a mink may kill a few muskrats, but considering the effort and risks involved in facing these big, well-armed rodents, the hunter is more inclined to seek safer prey—frogs, fish, mice. At the same time, the muskrat, with acres of open water, a variety of plant food available, can generally avoid exposing himself to mink, can avoid the land, and shallow water where he is most vulnerable to predation.

Winter changes these patterns, and the buffers between prey and predator are removed. As the frost, snow, and ice set in, many of the smaller prey of the mink go underground, underwater, into the mud, hide, hibernate, or migrate. The mink, no matter what the risks, must turn his attention to the muskrat, who cannot escape winter, stays on the marsh, stays active throughout the year. As the frost line lowers, the muskrat, like the mink, is faced with a decreasing number of food choices. There are fewer and fewer places left where he can get at plants, he must travel farther to find them, expose himself to a greater extent, and even, when winter becomes severe, leave the water and forage on the land. No matter what the risk from mink or other predators, the first requirement of the muskrat, as with all animals, is food, to survive.

Both the mink and the muskrat are in a sense forced to face each other directly by winter. In a way, the two species may be compared to military units. The muskrat population in a given wetland is a beleaguered army in a watery fortress. As food grows scarcer they must sally out into the open for supplies. When they do, they are vulnerable to the besiegers, the mink who persistently patrol, hunt, scout the edges, the shallows of the swampland.

Which muskrats will survive the siege of winter and mink is not entirely, or even largely, a matter of accident. If in the early fall of the year one were able to observe the members of a muskrat colony carefully enough, it would be possible to pick out certain animals whose chances of being alive the next spring were poor. It is the fringe members of the colony who are most vulnerable to the elements and predators. Very young (members of litters born

late in the season), very old, weakened, diseased, crippled animals are not good bets to survive. They are less able to find food and endure hardship than stronger animals, more likely to be driven away from food by sounder members of the colony.

In any colony or group of animals there are always such marginal members. The situation can best be explained through a hypothetical example. Let us suppose that there is a swamp which during the summer can support 125 muskrats, but can only support 100 animals through the winter. Which 25 members of the colony are excess, marginal, is not decided by reason, or even entirely by chance, but by a combination of natural factors of which predation, in this case the hunting activities of mink, is an important one.

In this imaginary winter pond, with 25 extra muskrats, some of the animals will be forced into less desirable, less safe portions of the territory. They will be so forced directly, because they are looking for food, or indirectly, by the stronger members of the colony who are not willing to share food. In any event they will end up foraging in areas where food supplies are poor, sheltering themselves in exposed locations. Some may even leave the main pond, attempt to live in shallow, nearby ponds. Subtle factors, slight physical or even psychological flaws—will normally determine which animals are driven to the margins of the territory. Sometimes it appears that what might be called social reasons determine which animals are marginal. Dr. Errington wrote that unattached, unmated male muskrats seemed to be particularly restless, and were among the first to leave the relative safety of the central swamp and set off overland, foraging, perhaps looking for new territories, mates of their own.

So far as they concern mink and predation, Dr. Errington's observations indicate that the marginal muskrats were the first to fall victim to mink. These were the easiest animals for the mink to catch, since they wandered to or were living in the most exposed locations; they were the easiest animals to kill, since they tended to be weaker and in many ways less efficient than the muskrats who remained in the heartland of the colony. All of which—i.e., that stronger (in various senses) animals are more likely to survive in a crisis than weaker ones—may be somewhat easier to understand than the claim made earlier that mink preying on these marginal muskrats is a constructive thing, good not only for the mink but for muskrats.

In explaining this statement it should first be pointed out that if there were no mink (or no other predators) besieging our imaginary 125-in-the-summer, 100-in-the-winter pond, some of the 25 marginal muskrats would be able to survive the winter. However, and this is a critical point in understanding the constructive nature of all predation, it would not be good for the muskrat population if these marginal, excess animals did survive. In terms of many muskrats, mink, swamps, many winters, the muskrat colony will be a stronger, healthier, more enduring one if these marginal animals are killed by mink than if they escape and continue to occupy the territory.

Why? How does a mink killing a muskrat help muskrats? As a first step in solving this apparent puzzle let us again look at our imaginary swamp. If only 100 animals are going to be able to survive the winter, then 25 of the fall population are, in a sense, living-dead. They are alive in the fall but they are doomed—they will not see the spring. However, the muskrats do not know which among them are marked for death. None of the animals is aware of his fate. Each individual will struggle to survive as long as he can. In a very real sense they will struggle, not against mink, but against the other muskrats. The 25 doomed animals will, for example, continue to eat, use up the food resources so long as they live. As a result of the 25 extra animals living and eating through the early part of the winter, there may not be food for even the 100 left at the end of the winter, and perhaps only 75 animals will survive. The 25 extra animals will themselves have died but in their prolonged struggle to live will have indirectly killed 25 other members of the colony who might otherwise have survived.

The role of the mink, the value of the predators for the muskrat colony is this. A mink will kill a muskrat quicker than starvation, exposure or disease does. The mink will kill some of the extra muskrats before they have a chance to kill members of their own colony. The mink protect muskrats from their own worst enemies, which are other muskrats.

To understand the value of predation it is important to remember that among all animals the fiercest competition is between members of the same species—between muskrats and muskrats —rather than between members of different species—mink and muskrats. Animals of the same kind need exactly the same kind of food, shelter, nesting areas, mates, and these resources are limited. When there are more animals trying to live in an area than there are resources available, the competition between them becomes disastrous. Some will die of starvation, as one takes food from another. Others will die of exposure, driven from protected territories by their own kind. Cannibalism may occur. Dr. Errington noted that desperate muskrats would turn savagely upon each other. Overcrowded, overcompetitive colonies are especially vulnerable to epidemic diseases, infestations of parasites. Finally, overpopulation and severe competition seem to create social problems. Surrounded by too many of their own kind, animals become abnormally aggressive, irritable, may not mate readily, bear fewer and weaker young, sometimes fail to care for their litters, or may even destroy them.

Preventing muskrats from destroying muskrats, either directly or indirectly, is a fundamental constructive service mink perform for muskrats, and one which all predators perform for all prey. Predators alone do not determine how many animals may live in a given territory, but predation is one force which contributes to maintaining optimum population levels and preventing overpopulation crises.

The notion that predation is beneficial in this regard, that mink protect muskrats from other muskrats, is not just a theory. There have been many actual examples which demonstrate the constructive role of the predators. One of the best known occurred some years ago in the Kaibab Forest, a wilderness area of 700,000 acres in the high plateau country of Arizona. This region was considered prime deer hunting territory. However, state game officials estimated that while the deer population was about 15,000, there was enough room and food in the Kaibab to support 30,000 head of deer. It was decided that the principal reason for there being fewer deer than there might be was that there were too many large predators—mountain lions, wolves, coyotes—feeding on the deer. Since deer hunting is not only a recreation for many, but economically important to those who supply hunters, it was decided to reduce the number of wild hunters who were killing deer that hunters would like to kill.

Professional hunters and trappers were encouraged and paid to eliminate the predators, and they did an efficient job. Some 7,000 coyotes, more than 700 lions and a number of wolves were killed in the Kaibab. At first the results seemed to be exactly as desired. Ten years after the antipredator campaign began, the deer population had increased to 30,000, supposedly the proper number for the area. However the deer population, no longer under pressure from the predators, did not remain at this ideal figure, but multiplied rapidly. The herd increased to 40,000 twelve years after the experiment began and jumped to 100,000 during the next two years. Shortly, the deer had used up all the territory and food in the Kaibab. The hungry, desperate animals frantically stripped the forest of every bit of forage. During the next two winters 40,000 deer died of starvation and disease. Eventually only about 10,000 remained, and many of the survivors were in poor condition.

In the Kaibab Forest the value of the original predators became apparent after the fact of the calamitous experiment. The predators had provided a sort of biological friction, a brake, which slowed down the rate of increase for the deer population. When the wild hunters were eliminated, the brake was released; the deer population ran wild, and eventually crashed in a dreadful biological accident. Not only did thousands of deer die in the disaster, but for many years afterward the effects of the experiment were felt in the area. During the period of peak population, the deer had, after regular food supplies were exhausted, made extraordinary efforts to stay alive, dug up roots, girdled trees. This in turn exposed the slopes to erosion, further denuding the land. As a result, even after the deer population in the Kaibab had dropped below its former level, food remained scarce and it took some years before the land was regenerated. The predators had been a factor not only in saving deer from other deer, but in saving the land itself (and thus many other smaller species) from deer.

In addition to helping control the numbers of prey species, predators help to control the quality of prey populations. This function can be explained by returning again to Dr. Errington's studies of mink and muskrats struggling to survive in frozen prairie swamps. According to Dr. Errington's observations, the animals most likely to be taken by the mink were muskrats that in one way or another were defective. They were the weaker animals, the diseased ones, those who were perhaps a bit slower, a bit less intelligent or adaptable than the average. Some of these animals may have been defective by accident or through injury, but it is probable that many of them carried some inherited flaw. Had these animals not been eliminated they would have presumably bred the next spring and by doing so passed on their deficient characteristics to their offspring, thus making the whole colony a little less fit.

In killing these animals, the mink unintentionally act in the same way as a scientific rancher or poultry man who culls his stock, eliminating the least desirable animals from the breeding population. This is the way the farmer improves the quality of his herd or flock and in the same way, the mink improves the quality of a muskrat colony. This is not, of course, the objective of the mink. He is only interested in getting the easiest meal possible, but because the easiest prey is often the least desirable genetically, the effect of predation is the same as that of scientific culling.

The old expression "survival of the fittest" applies in all these matters. The mink serves the muskrat colony by destroying many of its most unfit members. He protects fit members of the colony from the competition of unfit animals and he protects future muskrat generations from the danger of inheriting the characteristics of the defective animals, characteristics that would decrease the chances of the colony and, in the long run, of the species, surviving.

In later chapters, other beneficial effects of predation will be discussed. However, before leaving mink and muskrats, mountain lions and deer, I would like, because it is so important to an understanding and appreciation of the role of all predators, to re-emphasize the fundamental constructive value of the predator in the natural system. When we look at one predator, a mink, killing one muskrat, the act seems to be destructive. However, when we consider the competition between the two species we see that this is a constructive, in fact cooperative, relationship. Both contribute something to the welfare of the other. The prey feeds the predator; the predator protects the prey from its own kind.

This cooperative competition has existed throughout much of the natural history of the world. It is at the heart of the system by which life supports life. Since we know no other, it is impossible to say what might have happened if this system did not exist, if there had been no predators. However, because predation has so importantly influenced the number, kinds, and location of animals in the world, it is safe to assume that without this phenomenon, life, if it existed at all, would be vastly different from what it is today.

The Badger

All bears, dogs, cats have arrived (by the long, slow evolutionary route) at much the same solution to the basic problem of every living thing: survival. A bear in Alaska, a bear in Asia, a cat in Bengal and a cat in Brazil have much the same equipment, habits, niches, prey. In appearance they show a strong family resemblance. However, as has been mentioned, with the Mustelidae it is much different. Very few members of the family look alike, have the same habits or the same adaptations. In a sense (a fantastical one because no species, including our own, plans or controls its shape and character) the Mustelidae are like players who have made a number of original and clever moves in trying to hold their own in the complicated game of evolutionary chess in which we all take part.

The smallest of the clan—the weasels and mink—might be considered the most conventional of the family, the basic mustelids. They have come up with no tricks, no obvious specialties. They depend for survival upon being a bit quicker, more agile and persistent than the animals they prey upon and those that prey upon them. After these two small hunters the family becomes more curious, more various. It is hard, for example, to think

66

of the badger as a close relative of the weasel. Although they are both aggressive hunters, the likenesses are not obvious. The badger is a heavyset, flat, even fat animal with precious little chance of running down a rabbit, less chance still of squeezing down a rabbit's burrow.

Like so many other larger members of the Mustelidae who have become specialists, the badger, in the game of survival, has staked a lot on one ingenious move (in the chess sense), one adaptation (in the evolutionary sense). This animal's whole style of life, not just his hunting style, depends largely on a single talent: his ability to dig bigger, better holes, and dig them more rapidly than any other hunting mammal and most other mammals of any kind.

The digging skill of a badger is one of those natural phenomena, like the Grand Canyon or a tropical storm, that has to be seen to be believed, and even then the performance seems incredible. The first time I saw a badger at work was again when I was a boy living in southern Michigan. Michigan even then marked the easternmost edge of the badger's range. They were uncommon animals and now, I am told nonexistent in that part of the state. However, and this was thirty-five years ago, we did have one notable encounter with badgers.

My grandfather owned a nine-hole public golf course built on a sandy quarter section of land a half mile inland from the lakeside house where I lived. The golf course, though made for games, might also have been made for badgers. The fairways and greens were open, imitation prairies. The soil was light and dry, ideal for digging. Finally, the course swarmed with gophers (thirteen lined spermophiles), a little ground squirrel regarded by all proper badgers as a great delicacy.

One year a sow badger (the males are called boars, a nickname that gives some clue as to the general appearance of these unweasel-like animals) appeared. She may have moved to the golf course the previous fall, but nobody was aware of her until spring, when a series of big holes were found along the seventh fairway. My grandfather and father both had a lively interest in wildlife and, as amateur naturalists, enjoyed seeing the badger, since none had been living in the area for some years. However, as operators of a golf course, they did not enjoy the animal at all. Hole diggers of all sorts are the bane of greenskeepers. Even the gophers, who if left alone could make a green look like a Swiss cheese, honeycombed with half-dollar size burrows, were a problem. A badger who could make a fairway look as if an army had entrenched there was more in the nature of a disaster than just a problem.

It was decided without much debate that, interesting as she was, the badger would have to go. However, because she was rare, because she might have young (I was promised and eventually got one of these), and because of the general outlook of my family, it was decided that rather than shoot her, which would have been easy, we would catch her alive and send her to a zoo. This was not easy.

On the day of the great badger hunt my father, a greenskeeper named Ken, and myself set out for the seventh fairway in a pickup truck carrying shovels, a canvas tarpaulin, a wooden box, and my muskrat-shy airedale, Mike. We parked and waited downwind from the badger's main burrows. After a time she appeared, sniffed the air, sunned for a time and then waddled off, probably looking for a gopher. We started toward her as fast as the truck

68

would go. She doubled back toward the den but between Ken, who was in his spare time a motorcycle racer, driving the truck and Mike yapping excitedly, we cut her off from her burrow. Surrounding the animal, we hoped to throw the tarp over her and hold her long enough to get her in the box. The badger, however, was not cooperative. As we closed in she put her head down and began to dig, throwing up fairway turf and sandy loam behind her in a great geyser. Mike came up first and apparently got a hold on her tail, but she just kept digging and disappeared, leaving the dog with a mouthful of badger bristles.

Next we started after her with shovels, which was a hopeless job. Two men, a boy and a dog are, when it comes to digging, simply not in a badger's class. We dug a ten foot tunnel in what seemed like record time but by the sounds ahead we lost, so to speak, a lot of ground. The badger was farther away than when we started. We stopped, panting, and leaned on our shovels to reconsider our strategy. Ken, a very competitive man, suggested we get the tractor and go after the badger with a bulldozer blade. However, my father, pointing out that the object of the whole hunt was to save the seventh fairway, across which we had already cut a sizable trench, vetoed this idea. There was some talk about trying to get Mike down the hole, but the airedale did not seem to have much enthusiasm for this plan. Eventually we got the small portable pump that was used as an auxiliary to the sprinkling system, put it in a nearby pond, attached a length of two-inch hose and began to flood the badger's tunnel. By and by (many, many gallons later) the water caught up with the badger, she surfaced, spluttering, and we caught her in the tarp.

Normally badgers do not engage in competitive digging matches, there being few creatures foolish enough to challenge them in this way, but I have always remembered the morning on the golf course as an example of what a badger can do if pushed. However, even under ordinary circumstances, the abilities of this animal are impressive. I once watched a badger waddle up to a gopher hole (gophers themselves are accomplished tunnelers), start digging and then two minutes later appear with a gopher in her mouth. By poking sticks into the excavation I estimated that the badger had pursued the gopher through the ground at the rate of about three feet a minute.

Their remarkable skill as diggers most obviously serves the badgers as a specialized hunting technique. Like the other members of the Mustelidae, the badgers have a wide variety of prey. (They are also more inclined than the weasels to feed on carrion of all sorts.) Mice, moles, ground birds and their eggs, lizards, snakes (in the West, where they are most common, badgers have been observed preying on rattlesnakes), insects, grubs, as well as some plants are all eaten by badgers. They have also been known to feed on other members of their own family, occasionally digging out a litter of weasels or hibernating skunks. However, the bulk of the badger's diet consists of rabbits and ground squirrels, gophers, woodchucks, marmots and especially prairie dogs. There is nothing strategic or sly about the way badgers take most of these rodents. They simply find their burrow and dig out their prey.

Their excavating talent is also put to nonhunting uses. The home of a badger is the most elaborate made by any predator. Left undisturbed, badgers will create a maze of tunnels, including enlarged underground rooms for sleeping, eating, caching carrion. Unlike most of the other Mustelidae, badgers are relatively social animals, several generations sometimes inhabiting the same series of tunnels. So long as food supplies remain ample, young badgers will stay in the colony, and as the family grows, the underground quarters will be enlarged. The European badger, which is smaller but similar to the American, is particularly communal. The tunnels of one colony may sprawl out over two or three acres.

Also, unlike the weasels who carry little fat and must remain perpetually active in search of food, the badgers do get fat, in fact often are. In consequence, and also because they frequently drag carcasses underground for storage, badgers tend to disappear into their tunnel homes in bad weather and stay there until things improve. Badgers are not true hibernators but in the winter will sleep for long periods of time.

Young badgers are born in the late spring, far underground in dry grass-carpeted rooms. There are usually three or four young in a litter. Unlike the weasels and mink, male badgers seem to take little interest in the young, apparently do not help the females hunt for them or lead the young on educational hunting expeditions. One possible explanation is that young badgers do not have as much need for the services of two parents as do young mink or weasels. Weasels, for example, have a variety of hunting techniques and skills that they must learn, and in many ways they must hunt harder, oftener than badgers to survive. Once a young badger has dug up one or two ground squirrels, he has learned much of what he needs to know.

Like all young animals, new-born badgers are potentially vulnerable to other predators, but in fact they are probably among the safest of all young creatures. Except for an occasional curious man, there are few other animals who could get at an underground nest of badgers. Further, even if they could reach the young, hardly any animals, except perhaps a bear, would dare to try to force their way into a badger den guarded by an adult female.

Badgers are as fierce, aggressive and pugnacious as the weasels, but in addition they are about fifty times as large, old adults weighing up to twenty pounds. Badgers may be described as fearless because in the normal course of events they seldom meet anything they need to fear. As an illustration of how badgers regard the rest of the world, mother badgers, escorting young animals on hunting trips, have been known, while crossing roads, to challenge automobiles that seem to be threatening their young.

The badger has the same slashing, shearing teeth as the weasel, but they are much larger, the jaws much stronger. Perhaps its most formidable defensive weapons are the powerful shoulders and enormous front claws. These are, of course, principally digging tools (a badger's forepaw is about the size of a man's hand), but if he must, a badger will deliver a raking, tearing swipe with his claws. There is still another adaptation of the badger which serves as a defensive device. Badgers have a thick coarse coat and a sloppy appearance, as if they were wearing a hand-me-down hide that originally belonged to a much larger animal. This is not an illusion. The badger's skin is not only very tough but it is very loose. Many a dog who has rashly grabbed a badger by his hindquarters has learned to his sorrow that these animals come close to being able to turn around in their own hide. Though staging fights between badgers and specially bred dogs was once a popular entertainment in Ireland and England, these matches were artificial ones in which the badger was at a considerable disadvantage. So far as the larger American badger is concerned, I have never seen a dog that I would bet on against a badger. I have, however, seen the remains of several dogs who, unfortunately, tried to become badger killers.

In the wild, a few young badgers may be surprised and taken by eagles or coyotes. Under special circumstances, wolves, bobcats, or mountain lions may take an adult animal, but this would be a rare occurrence. While there are few observations of larger hunters preying on badgers, there is one persistent story, reported by many reliable outdoorsmen, of a special, cooperative relationship between badgers and one of the other predators, the coyote. The story is that the badger and the coyote (who often shares the badger's range and his taste for rodents) will sometimes establish a hunting partnership. Individual badgers and coyotes are reported to have regularly hunted together on a more than accidental basis. Each brings to the partnership something the other lacks. The coyote will chase a rabbit or a ground squirrel down a hole. The badger waddles along behind until he reaches the den, then proceeds to dig out the prey. Sometimes the rodent will flee past the digging badger, and the waiting coyote will grab it. Other times the badger gets the prize. Who gets the meal depends upon circumstances and luck, not agreement, but observers of this peculiar partnership agree that the two hunters do not seem to quarrel over the spoils. Sometimes they have been seen to feed almost side by side without hostility. An etymological sidelight to this arrangement suggests that it is both a common and long-standing one. *Talcoyote,* meaning "like a coyote," is a Mexican Indian name for the badger. Since a badger and coyote do not remotely resemble one another physically, perhaps the name was given because of their predatory partnership.

Though the badger is a relatively large, well-armed animal whose underground habits give him great security from natural enemies, he is becoming everywhere in the United States less numerous. East of the Mississippi he is very rare now. In the Great Plains states, the heartland of his range, he is much less common than he once was. Again the reason for his decline can be to a large measure traced to the activities of man.

Direct human predation is a factor, but not a major one, explaining the decrease in the badger population. By and large, badgers are among the best-liked of the mustelids. They seldom if ever are a direct threat to domestic stock, having little inclination for raiding chicken coops, and as a rule do not live in areas where poultry is commonly raised. Furthermore, their obvious preference for rodents, known to ranchers to be destructive, is a factor in their favor. From the standpoint of western farmers and ranchers, the only undesirable trait of the badger is his hole-digging habit. Occasionally a horse or cow will stumble in a badger tunnel and injure himself. Because of such incidents a landowner will now and then poison or shoot badgers.

Badgers, like all the Mustelidae, have some value as furbearers. Badger fur once was popular as trim for coat collars and cuffs. At one time, stiff, bristly badger hairs were in demand for shaving and other brushes. However, nowadays plastic bristles are preferred for this use. By and large, badgers were never as valuable furbearers as some of the other members of the family, and the value has declined to the point where trapping cannot be considered an important threat to the animal.

As is the case with many native animals, the badger has been most, and most adversely, affected by man because of the way in which we have altered his environment and his relations with other animals. In the most obvious way we have tended to turn thousands of acres of land that was once good badger country into poor badger country. For example, though Michigan was never prime badger country, being too close to forested areas, the fate of the badger on our golf course is an example of this situation. In the 1930s our golf course was a good environment for badgers, but we would not permit them to use it. Today the golf course is no more; it was converted into a housing development twenty years ago. There are few places left where a badger could live (gophers have all but disappeared) and even if he could, the increase in the human population would make the area uninviting. The same situation exists in many other areas where men, for good or bad, necessary or unnecessary reasons, have occupied wildlife ranges and converted them to their more or less exclusive use.

Secondly, and perhaps even more importantly in an environmental sense, men have contributed to the decline of the badger by reducing the number and range of the prey species upon which the badger is most dependent. As the mink has a special and close relationship with the muskrat, so does the badger with another medium-sized rodent, the prairie dog. Traditionally, badgers were always abundant in and about prairie-dog towns. It is an obvious relationship. Both animals are diggers, both thrive in light, easily excavated soil. Prairie dogs are an ideal size for a badger to prey upon. In return, a badger is an ideal animal to protect (as the mink protects muskrats) prairie dogs from overpopulation.

In the early days of the West, the prairie dog was the commonest rodent in the Great Plains area, perhaps one of the most numerous animals on the continent. Ancient prairie-dog towns, mazes of runs, burrows, tunnels, stretched in some places for fifty or sixty miles and were inhabited by hundreds of thousands of these little rodents. Everywhere there were prairie dogs there were badgers, living in comparative ease, busy most of the time doing their part to ensure that there would not be too many prairie dogs.

Once the West was opened for agriculture, farmers and ranchers declared war on the prairie dog. (The details of this long engagement will be discussed in a later chapter dealing with the black-footed ferret, another mustelid who inhabited prairie-dog towns.) Prairie dogs, according to ranchers, tore up the ground with their holes, creating a physical hazard for men and domestic animals. Even more seriously, it was thought that the rodents ruined range grass by overgrazing, creating serious erosion problems. Therefore, with guns, fire, and particularly poison, individual ranchers, state and federal pest-control agents set about to reduce sharply, if not eliminate, prairie dogs. The campaign has been successful; prairie dogs, though not at the moment threatened with extinction, are everywhere much less numerous than they once were and have disappeared altogether from their former western range.

The badger, being so dependent upon these rodents, was in a sense an innocent victim caught up in the middle of the man *versus* prairie-dog war. Insofar as the fate of the badger depended upon that of the prairie dog, the decline of these hunters serves as a good illustration of another one of the fundamental principles of predation: predators help to control the numbers and quality of prey. Simultaneously, prey species, to an even greater extent, control the numbers and quality of the predators.

Particularly for one interested in predators, this is a most important principle to understand. There is a widespread and generally false assumption that left to their own devices predator animals would overcontrol the prey species valuable to man. This assumption explains, although it does not justify, the activities of many state game agencies who offer bounties on predators with the object of protecting game species from these wild hunters.

To illustrate this principle, we can again return to the imaginary prairie marsh in the winter and the relationship between the mink and muskrat. As we saw in the preceding chapter, the mink controlled the quantity and quality of the muskrat by preying upon, in most cases, the marginal members of the colony. However, simultaneously the muskrats were performing the same service for the mink, not by preying directly upon them, killing and eating them, but by refusing to be preyed upon, denying food to the mink.

The first mink to suffer when the hunting gets hard, when only the fittest muskrats are available, will be young, old, weakened, crippled, and otherwise defective animals. These will be the first to seek new and less desirable hunting grounds, where their difficulties will be multiplied and their chances of survival decreased. These marginal mink will, in theory, be the first to die, and it is to the long-range benefit of the mink population as a whole that they do.

Something similar to this imaginary situation between mink and muskrat is what actually occurred between badgers and prairie dogs. However, rather than being restricted to a few individuals in a single locality, the badger–prairie dog phenomenon involved thousands of individuals scattered across the whole central portion of North America. As the prairie dogs were shot, burned, and poisoned, as their vast towns were depopulated and abandoned, the badgers also disappeared. Now in reality, the badgers, once the prairie dogs began to decline, did not simply turn up their heels and die, no more than mink, in practice, did, when

muskrats became scarce. Individual animals moved to new territories, turned to new food sources, made every effort to continue to survive. However, throughout much of their range, the prairie dog was the best possible prey for the badger. When he was forced to turn elsewhere, hunting became harder; he was forced to expose himself to more risks; it became more difficult to breed; fewer young badgers were born; and fewer of those born survived.

All of this, the slow changes in animal populations caused by infinitely complex relationships between species, is commonly spoken of as the balance of nature. Though a popular one, it is a somewhat misleading phrase. It suggests a static, fixed relationship, that there is some perfect relationship between prey and predators—10 mink and 100 muskrats, or 500 badgers and 10,000 prairie dogs—which is perpetually maintained. The truth is that if we think of the balance of nature, we should think of a continually teetering one, which is always being adjusted, in which the only permanent factor is change. Between prey and predators there will be times when it appears that one or the other has the advantage, that the balance has shifted in their direction. This is illusionary, for when relationships seem most imbalanced, shifts and adjustments are taking place. If there are too many prey species for the land to support, predators will begin to invade the area, to breed more rapidly, survive more easily, and the balance will begin to swing in their direction. If the predators become too numerous, too efficient, prey will inevitably become scarcer, the predators will find survival more difficult, will have to move elsewhere or perish. As they do, their prey will have a chance to recover, become more numerous, stronger. If one admits the obvious, that predators and prey are not in conflict, but rather are dependent upon one another, then it is easy to understand how neither can completely dominate the other. Predators need prey to feed upon, and the prey need to be fed upon by predators for their own protection.

Normally, over a long period of years, the relationship between prey and predators will, while always shifting slightly, remain relatively stable. As between badgers and prairie dogs, mink and muskrats, population fluctuation will be slight in any given year. There will be as many prey animals as the land can efficiently support and as many predators as can be efficiently supported by the prey population. However, sometimes there are quick, radical shifts. Some new factor is introduced into the environment, the

80

relationship between species is suddenly changed, the balance will teeter wildly, and the results are almost always disastrous.

The killing of the big predators in the Kaibab Forest is one such example of extraordinary change, and there are many others. Several years ago, I spent a few weeks during the winter collecting plants with a botanist friend in Jamaica. This Caribbean island is a botanist's paradise, since in a small area it offers jungle, desert, seacoast, and alpine environments. However, it is a relatively dull place for people interested in mammals and birds. The reason is because of a disastrous breakdown in the normal prey-predator relationships. Some years ago, British coffee and sugar planters on the island became worried about snakes. (Ironically, so far as anybody knows, there were very few, if any, poisonous snakes on the island.) To combat the imagined danger from snakes, Asiatic mongooses were brought to Jamaica and released. The mongoose, made famous by Rudyard Kipling in his story "Rikki-Tikki-Tavi," is a member of the civet family, closely related to the Mustelidae. A mongoose looks and behaves, so far as his hunting goes, much like a medium-sized weasel. In Asia, the mongoose has a considerable and well-deserved reputation as a snake killer. However, these little animals do not restrict their hunting to snakes. They prey upon whatever is available.

Once introduced to Jamaica, the mongooses obligingly gobbled up the few snakes they found, but they did not stop there. The Caribbean islands have never, in recent times, been inhabited by large predators. Several small insectivores are the principal hunters. On the island, the mongoose had no competitors, no other predators with whom he had to share food, no larger hunters who could prey on him. Furthermore the native prey species were not prepared by inheritance (evolutionary adaptations) or experience to deal with these aggressive little Asiatic hunters. Mongooses have simply taken over the island. In the process they have destroyed most of the native small mammals, ground-nesting birds, and reptiles, and have turned to preying on domestic poultry and to scrounging in garbage dumps. When you walk through the forests of Jamaica you seldom see any small animals at ground level, except mongooses. These you see everywhere, and you also see them scuttling across porches, into office buildings, down streets.

This would seem to be an example of predation running wild, permanently altering the balance of nature. However, there is some indication that things may be changing. Though the mongoose is now so well established that nothing, including man, is likely to oust him directly, there are indications that one enemy may eventually control this imported predator—the enemy is of course other mongooses. My botanist friend said that though they were still numerous, the mongooses seemed to be declining in numbers, that there had been cases of epidemic-type diseases reported in the mongoose population. It may be that in time, disease, overcrowding, and lack of food will reduce the population to the point where some of the native fauna can make a comeback and learn how to cope with the invader.

Two predatory birds native to North America serve as another example of what can happen when normal prey-predator relations are disrupted. The Everglade kite and the California condor are two of the rarest birds in this country. Ornithologists estimate that there are fewer than twenty-five of the kites left alive, probably fewer than a hundred condors. Despite study and conservation projects by federal and state governments, the odds are that these two hunting birds will both become extinct during this century.

Many factors have brought them into this perilous position, but in both cases the basic problem has been a disruption of their traditional relationship with prey species.

The Everglade kite is, to put it mildly, a very finicky eater, having specialized to the point that it preys almost exclusively on one species of freshwater snail found in Florida swamps. The problem for this bird is that the best snail-producing swamps are being drained in order to make more land suitable for farming, homes, and industries. The kite has been pushed into a smaller and smaller area, food supplies have dwindled, the breeding rate of the birds has declined. The snails, in a sense, may well control the kite to the point of extinction.

With a ten-foot wingspan, the California condor is a huge, prehistoric-looking and in some ways prehistoric-acting bird. The time of the condor, exclusively a carrion eater, was centuries ago when great herds of game roamed the western plains and mountains. A by-product of the game herds were carcasses, animals that had died of disease or been pulled down by mammalian hunters. The condor is a big, slow-moving, unaggressive bird. To feed properly he needed a large carcass to gorge upon undisturbed. Once having fed, he could go some days before finding another suitably isolated carcass. However, in the last century, the game herds—buffalo and elk—have been displaced by domestic sheep and cattle. These supply some carcasses but not in the numbers that the wild herds did, since for a rancher the object is to keep his stock healthy, not to let it die on the open range and become condor food. In consequence, the range of these great birds has shrunk to a tiny area in the southern California mountains, and their numbers have dwindled to a pitiful handful.

In all of these examples—badgers and prairie dogs, mongooses in Jamaica, Everglade kites and their snails, condors and carcasses —the critical factor responsible for the wild and disastrous fluctuation in the natural balance has been some action of man that has drastically affected the environment and the natural prey-predator relationships.

These are typical, not exceptional examples. They are not cited to prove that man is wicked or animals persecuted, but only to show how complex the natural balance is, how durable under ordinary circumstances, how vulnerable under extraordinary conditions. The truth is that in modern times there has never been an example of a predator species overwhelming his prey, or vice versa, except when man has somehow destroyed the natural relationship between the two. Normally the destruction is unintentional. For example, Florida swamps were not drained to persecute the Everglade kite but to open land for human use. The fate of the kite was simply an accident, as has been that of the badger who has suffered because of the elimination of the prairie dog.

In the distant past, certain species have become extinct without any assistance from man. However, there is no record of the fundamental cause of extinction having been predation. What might be called natural extinction occurs when there is a cataclysmic shift in the environment, when grasslands become desert, deserts oceans, or temperate lands are covered with ice. In such periods of great environmental change, the final push into oblivion may be delivered by one species to another (as the snail may to the kite) but the prey-predator relation is never the underlying reason for the disaster.

This, of course, is not to suggest that because man can wreak havoc with the natural balance he should cease and desist in all his activities. We are part of nature too, and have the same urges and the same right to survival as any other creature. However, it should be remembered that in the last century or so we have come to possess enormous force, command energies that surpass those of glaciers, storms, floods. We must assume responsibility for the wise use of these forces and energy, not so much for the sake of a single species, say, the already doomed Everglade kite, but for the sake of all life on earth, for the sake of ourselves.

When, as we often have, we become enraged or alarmed over the activities of predators—badgers against prairie dogs, lions against deer, mink against muskrat—and demand that these predators be controlled or eliminated, we are, in a real sense, ignoring our own responsibilities. In regard to the predator-prey relation it must be remembered that no species has ever been hunted into extinction except by man. The balance may shift from time to time but it will continue to exist because predator and prey are mutually dependent. They cannot exist without each other, and therefore they continue to exist because of each other. They will continue to exist unless we men, with our awesome power, unintentionally or maliciously radically alter the environment within which the natural system operates, and thus destroy the delicate relationships between the species.

The Skunk

Of all the Mustelidae, the commonest in North America, the best known, and the best known for his special adaptation, is the skunk. There are three species in this country: the striped, hognose, and spotted. However, since they are all quite similar, most of what follows will deal with the striped skunk, the most numerous and widely distributed of the three animals.

The special adaptation of the skunk—his ability to eject a spray of evil-smelling liquid—is the most curious defensive mechanism of any mammal in the country. The liquid the skunk uses as, in a sense, ammunition is clear yellow in color, strongly acid in reaction. It is produced in a pair of anal glands. The glands are sheathed by a strong muscle which the skunk can voluntarily control, contract. The liquid is discharged through ducts which protrude from the anus when the skunk is ready to use his weapon. Normally these ducts are not visible. When the skunk becomes alarmed, judges it is time to take defensive action, he will raise his tail, the ducts will protrude, the muscles will contract and the liquid will be shot out in a fine mist, just as spray is produced when one squeezes the bulb of an atomizer or squirt gun. The skunk can aim this discharge with great accuracy and the spray can carry up to twelve feet.

The effect of the chemical discharge is considerable and spectacular. The stench is strong, acrid, highly offensive to almost all other creatures. Furthermore, once the spray saturates fur or clothing the odor will linger on for days. There is a common belief that if the spray is directed at close range into the eyes it will cause blindness. This is not true. The spray will cause the eyes to burn, create tears which may make it hard to see for a few minutes, but shortly the tears will have done their work and washed out the irritating liquid.

Though the skunk's weapon is nonlethal, in a sense humane, it is nonetheless extremely effective and gives the skunk very nearly absolute protection from enemies of all sorts. Few hunters, including man, will casually challenge a skunk. Large wild hunters, such as dogs, cats, the bigger Mustelidae, who are physically capable of preying on skunks, seldom do except in the most desperate circumstances. The only animals that regularly prey on skunks are the large birds of prey, chiefly the great horned owls, who are able to strike before the skunk can defend himself and who furthermore have no sense of smell, or only a rudimentary one.

Like the badger, with his special talent for digging, the skunk's adaptation has affected his entire style of life. However, the effect on the skunk has been indirect. The badger, for example, uses his powerful digging equipment as a direct tool in hunting, to create shelter as well as to protect himself. The chemical spray of the skunk is never used to catch prey, stun it.

Sometimes in discussions of international affairs, the expression "atomic shield" will be used. The notion is that countries possessing nuclear weapons are safe from attack because to attack them would involve enormous risks for the attacker. Thus, it is sometimes argued that the possession of nuclear arms, the most dreadful weapons ever invented, in fact insures peace. Whether this argument will prove to be true in regard to human affairs remains to be seen. (If false, few will be able to testify to the error of this theory.) However, so far as the skunk is concerned, there does seem to be some validity to the argument. The skunk lives and operates, largely in peace, behind his chemical shield. The heavy, often obese skunk waddles about the countryside, unhurriedly finding food, sleeping, rearing young in comparative security.

The skunk is one of the best examples of how a single important adaptation can affect an animal's physique and habits. To begin with there is the basic matter of color. The flashy black and white markings of the skunk make it the most conspicuous predator, one of the most conspicuous mammals of any sort. Nearly all other furbearers are plainly, drably marked; their coats serve as camouflage. Whether they are hunters or hunted, it is to their advantage to be inconspicuous. Ages ago, the forebear of the skunk may well have been such a plain-marked creature as the weasel. However, as the effective scent defense evolved, the color requirements of a skunk changed. A skunk has little to fear from any right-minded hunter who recognizes him. Just the fact that he is a skunk, can secrete the objectionable liquid, is enough to discourage all but the most desperate predators. (In the wild, skunks seldom actually use the spray. They have a few gestures, the stamping of their feet, lifting of the tail, which usually are sufficient warning.) What the skunk does want to avoid is being attacked by some ignorant, impetuous, inexperienced animal, say a young domestic dog, who does not know with whom he is deal-

ing. Therefore it is greatly to the skunk's advantage to be able to announce boldly, openly, that he is a skunk. It is likely that the black-and-white pattern of his markings evolved to serve this purpose.

Other obvious physical characteristics of the skunk, his stoutness, nearsightedness, waddling gait, may also have evolved, in part, for the same reason. Again, ages ago, the ancestors of skunks were probably weasel-like, being slimmer of body, quicker of foot, more energetic than the modern animal. However, once the chemical weapon was developed, skunks could afford to slow down, to stroll about in the open in relative peace and security. Not only could they do this, but it was to their advantage to do so. They were able to stop competing with the swifter, more energetic, aggressive hunters. Ambling over the countryside, examining their hunting territory in a very leisurely way, they came to fill a different niche, find different prey than was possible for weasel or mink, who lacked the skunk's almost invulnerable chemical shield. In the course of evolutionary time, as the chemical apparatus developed, the skunk's habits changed to aid his physical requirements. He became the slow-moving, shuffling animal we know because he could, and because this is the most efficient form for such a hunter.

The temperament of skunks has also been affected by their secure shield. Of all the Mustelidae, the skunk is the most even-tempered, placid, unexcitable. A skunk caught raiding a garbage can, for example, will seldom run away. He may look up, perhaps give a warning wave of his tail and go on about his business. A fox, raccoon, or opossum will scuttle away quickly. Walking down a path, encountering a bear, a skunk will continue on his way. It will be the bear who turns aside. The easygoing, sometimes arrogant attitude of the skunk toward his environment makes him a particularly easy animal to observe, and I have always thought a particularly charming one. The skunk I knew best was a male who lived with my wife and me in an apartment in Washington. His name was Irving and we got him shortly after we were married and moved to the city. Irving was two or three months old when we got him, and descented. It is possible to keep skunks without performing the simple operation that removes the scent-producing gland. However, living with a "natural" skunk, particularly in a rented apartment, can be risky.

Young skunks make good housepets, being playful after the manner of a kitten, easily housebroken, reasonably affectionate and easy to care for, since they will eat and thrive on table scraps. Since my wife and I were both working, there was another advantage to keeping a skunk. They are largely nocturnal and fit into a routine such as ours was then. When we left the apartment in the morning, Irving was sleeping and usually was still sleeping when we returned. In the evening he was ready to be sociable.

Living with Irving for several years gave us a fairly good understanding of a skunk's rather well-developed ego. For example, his food dish was in the corner of a tiny dinette. When, as was occasionally unavoidable, one of us got between the skunk and his dinner plate he would not, as a less self-important, confident animal might, go around us or between our legs. He would stop and stamp his feet commandingly until we got out of his way. Foot stamping is an inherited habit of skunks. It is actually a communicative sign. It means just what it seems to mean: "Get out of my way." It also means, "if you don't get out of my way I may have to move you with a little spray." Irving, of course, could not follow through on the threat, but he did not know this and so habitually stamped his feet as a fully-armed skunk would.

In the late evening we would put a cat harness on Irving and take him for a walk around the downtown Washington block where we lived. The walks were very slow ones since skunks are not only slow but curious, like all the Mustelidae. He would find in the course of a block innumerable objects to be sniffed, examined, considered. Occasionally we would meet other apartment dwellers walking their dogs. Left alone, Irving paid very little attention to the dogs, giving the impression that he regarded them as unimportant, unworthy creatures. However, sometimes an excited dog came too close, became too aggressive. Then Irving would halt, fluff out like an enraged tomcat and majestically raise the plume of his tail, giving the final warning. In Irving's case this was a bluff, but this is one of the principal functions of the gesture, to warn away the misguided, make it unnecessary to use the ultimate weapon.

A wild, fully-equipped skunk out hunting in the night will behave very much as Irving did walking around a city block. A skunk will set out from his den and ramble several miles during the course of a night. It is almost impossible to list what a skunk may find to eat during the course of an evening's stroll. They are omnivorous animals and their tastes are much more varied than any of the other Mustelidae. To begin with, they eat many sorts of roots, tubers, fruits, and other plants. Raspberries, blackberries, elderberries, nuts, corn are all favored by skunks. In the animal line almost anything is a potential meal for a skunk. Insects are a favorite: grubs, earthworms, beetles, bees (including, if they should find them, the larvae and honey of the bees) and many others are eaten. Next to the badgers, the skunks are perhaps the best diggers among the Mustelidae, having long, strong front claws and strong shoulders. In their rambles skunks are forever digging, pulling apart, tearing into things, looking for food. Among other animals skunks prey on all manner of small amphibians, reptiles, and when they can find them in shallow water, fish. Skunks are very fond of eggs—turtle eggs, snake eggs, eggs of ground-nesting birds, including those of domestic hens when they are available. In the mammalian line skunks again will eat what they can find. They will dig out ground squirrels, destroy a nest of young rabbits, and presumably, if they could find them, a litter of young weasels. Like the other Mustelidae, mice are the mammal most frequently preyed upon by the skunk. Though slow-footed, skunks are well-coordinated, quick animals. They also have very good hearing and depend upon this sense perhaps to a greater degree than other mustelids. Hunting in a field, a skunk will shuffle quietly along, hear a rustle in the grass and pounce on a mouse much as a cat will.

By and large, the feeding habits of a skunk have made him popular in agricultural areas. Occasionally a skunk may make a habit of taking eggs or even chickens from a hen house, but this is not common and since skunks are more easily shot or trapped than the quick weasels, their destruction of domestic poultry can be easily controlled. Hunters and sportsmen sometimes complain that skunks are a menace to game birds, destroying their nests and young, but again in comparison to the complaints lodged against other predators, this is a mild one. Generally farmers, knowing that the skunk feeds largely on crop-destroying insects and rodents, have a high regard for the skunk. In Michigan, when I was growing up, there were nests of skunks under many barns and sheds, and the owners, unless they were in the poultry business, were glad to have the little catlike hunters there. In New York

State the skunk is now a protected animal, and legislation giving him this status was initiated by growers of hops who knew skunks often fed on a grub that was especially fond of their vines.

Like the badger, the skunk will often feed on carrion and sometimes will drag a carcass underground and store it. Being fat, even fatter than the badger, the skunk can, if he must, go for considerable periods without eating. This is often the case in the winter in bad weather. Again, skunks are not true hibernators, but as the weather becomes colder they will become drowsier and will sleep days on end. Several female skunks and young animals will often be found sleeping together in a den during the winter, and this is one situation where they are vulnerable to predation by dogs, coyotes, cats, their own larger relatives such as badgers.

Adult male skunks seem to remain more active during the winter, and toward the end of the winter begin to travel widely in search of mates. When two or more males with this objective meet, they will often fight. Interestingly, these scuffles are hand-to-hand combats so to speak. Neither animal uses his scent weapon.

Young skunks are born in the spring and early summer with half a dozen young being average for a litter. For nesting and hibernation, skunks may dig their own den or use that of a woodchuck or rabbit. They also frequently get under the foundations of a building and may sometimes be found in hollow logs. Young skunks stay underground for a month or so, then they begin to follow their mother on hunting-learning expeditions. Often little skunks will follow the female (males do not assume responsibility in this matter) in single file. Such a line of the little black-and-white hunters marching sedately down a path is one of the most charming sights in the woods.

Family groups, mother and young, will sometimes remain together into the winter, but otherwise skunks are not social animals in the sense that dogs with their pack organization are. However, except as noted during mating season, skunks are not quarrelsome and seem to share hunting ranges without much trouble. One reason may be that, because they are omnivorous, because hunting is relatively easy for them, there is not the competitive pressure between skunks that there is, for example, between weasels.

Ten years ago I, along with a number of other naturalists, was able to observe a curious phenomenon which involved many skunks and, in fact, many predators. In the Virginia countryside, twenty-five miles from Washington, D.C., the federal government bought a considerable tract of farmland to serve as a site for the new Dulles International Airport. There was a lag of almost two years between the time the land was purchased, the farmers moved away, and the beginning of construction on the landing strips and terminal buildings.

Almost as soon as farming operations ceased there was an explosion of rodents, meadow voles, house mice, woods mice, rats. In many of the old barns grain had been abandoned and there were crops still in the field. Barn cats had gone, as had the men who would normally be interested in trapping or poisoning the rodents. In late summer the fields of what now is Dulles Airport were literally alive with mice and other rodents. Everywhere you walked you saw, heard, even smelled them.

In the fall there began an invasion of predators which enabled naturalists who were fortunate enough to be in the area to have literally a field day. At the time I was particularly interested in the birds of prey, and in those fields we had a chance to observe winged hunters in such numbers and variety as we had never seen before. There were sparrow hawks, pigeon hawks, peregrines, Cooper's hawks, sharpshins, goshawks, red-tails, red-shouldered, rough-legged hawks, as well as half a dozen species of owls. On the ground there were foxes, weasels, raccoons, even an occasional bobcat, and more numerous than any other, the skunks. Day after day all spent their time gobbling up mice and rats. Once, early in the morning, standing at the edge of a twenty-acre field, I saw seven skunks mousing in the stubble.

One question that came to my mind then, and has occurred to me since, is how do the predators know when such a situation has occurred, how do they know to go to an area where for special reasons food is temporarily abundant. The reverse situation—predators leaving an area when food is scarce—is fairly easy to figure out. They leave because they must. They have very hard times, may perhaps even starve if they stay. But how they find places like the abandoned farms is a more difficult question. Animals are not able to communicate such information to each other and even if they could, probably would not since each individual is concerned with his own survival, not that of his kin.

My own answer can perhaps be illustrated by again using a military-political phrase which is currently popular, the domino theory. Let us assume that in the area around the fields that now are Dulles Airport there were territories inhabited by a hundred skunks. Directly in the area of the abandoned fields there were ten skunks, farther out another ten and so on, until you came to the final ten, living ten miles away (far outside a skunk's normal traveling range) from the fields. When the mice began to multiply, the nearest skunks moved directly into the fields. In doing so they abandoned part of their regular territory. The ten skunks next in line would soon discover this in their prowling. It would not be an intentional discovery. It would simply be a situation in which they

found, so to speak, open hunting. They would continue to move toward the fields that were teeming with mice because other hunters had vacated the land. In the same way, skunks in the next tier of territories would begin to move toward the mice-loaded fields. Eventually the effect, the shift in hunting grounds, might be felt by the animals ten miles away and they in time would tend to press into the area of abundance. As a row of dominoes will fall one after another (or as a row of nations are said to fall unless the first is propped up), so the skunks, in a sense, fell into the good hunting area.

The whole situation was a very temporary, abnormal one. By the next spring the number of rodents had decreased markedly in the old fields and so had the number and variety of predators who had contributed to the decline of the rodents. Shortly thereafter, construction on the new jetport began and the environment was no longer suitable either for prey or predators.

Though no accurate census of nongame animals exists, the guess of most naturalists is that the skunk is the most numerous animal customarily called predatory in the country. Furthermore, the guess also is that skunks are many times more numerous than they ever have been before. The reason for this is much the same as the reason for the abnormal scarcity of other animals, the badger, for example. It can be traced to the activities of man, his environment-changing faculty.

Prior to the coming of the Europeans to the North American continent, the skunk was probably a relatively numerous animal. Not having many natural enemies, being a reasonably rapid breeder, it was very likely a common predator. However, before the Europeans began to change the nature of the land, there was much less land than there now is that might be considered prime skunk territory. The skunk hunts, thrives best in relatively open land or land in which the cover is not thick. Originally much of the continent was covered with relatively heavy forest, which is something less than ideal for skunks.

Just as we have unintentionally brought the Everglade kite to the verge of extinction by draining swamps for our own use, we have unintentionally created millions of new acres of good skunk territory by clearing the forests, opening the land. Not only have we given skunks a lot of open agricultural land to forage in but we have created new food sources for him with our domestic crops and the insects and rodents which feed on them. Finally, since he is adaptable, omnivorous, and secure, the skunk has become a scavenger of man. Skunks are common today throughout many of the suburban, even urban areas of the country where they can get along quite well on the food scraps we create, and where they can find shelter under our buildings.

Skunk is among the least valuable of all the mustelid furs, but it is common and there has always been some market for it, thus some trapping. In the 1920s and 1930s, fashion designers used many more skunk pelts than they do today. Trapping pressure increased and also many people began raising skunks in captivity. When the styles changed, trapping pressure was reduced. Additionally, when the fur price dropped, many skunk ranchers went out of business and when they did, simply opened their pens and let the caged animals go wild. Today skunks are still trapped in some numbers, but trapping obviously is not a serious threat to the animals, since their numbers are steadily increasing.

In some states bounties are offered on skunks because it is assumed they are a threat to game and domestic animals, but again this is not a major matter. The automobile probably destroys more skunks than any other device or habit of man. Being slow, relatively unafraid, nocturnal scavengers, inhabitants of open places, skunks are particularly apt to be traffic victims as can be observed by any motorist.

However, to repeat, the overall effect of human activities on the continent has been to increase the number of skunks, to have, in a sense, given them an artificial advantage. All of which brings up some obvious questions: What of the so-called balance of nature?

Is it possible that we will be overwhelmed by skunks as Jamaica was overwhelmed by the mongoose? How will they be controlled?

My own feeling is that we certainly have enough skunks now, perhaps too many. As to control, I think it has gone beyond the point where another wild species will readjust the balance in regard to the skunk. Other predators are not much of a threat nor are the direct activities of man—hunting them for bounties, trapping them, running over them on the highway. Furthermore, the prey species—rodents, insects—probably will not control skunks, since they are so adaptable in their feeding habits and men have created new, artificial skunk food.

Predicting the future is a risky business, but just as speculation, I believe that skunks will be controlled, that in the next several decades their numbers will decline. The skunks will be controlled by the only creature capable of doing so, other skunks. There is already evidence that this may be the case. In the eastern United States where skunks are most, perhaps excessively, plentiful, there have in the past ten years been increased reports of rabies among these animals. As more and more skunks attempt to inhabit smaller and smaller areas the likelihood of this and other epidemic diseases reducing their numbers increases.

Several fur-buyer acquaintances tell me that, without having kept precise records, they have the distinct feeling that during the past decades pelts brought to them indicate that skunks in general seem to be smaller, less healthy than they were in the early part of the century. This seems a reasonable observation. The more numerous the animals, the larger the number of defectives in the population, the more inbreeding will take place. Also social relations between skunks are likely to become more strained. The animals will become more irritable toward each other, may produce smaller, less healthy litters. All of which indicates that skunks against skunks will tend to decrease the population.

Finally, I have the feeling that the increased use of pesticides may have a drastic effect on the skunks. Despite much controversy, no one is absolutely certain how serious the side effects of insecticide use are for other forms of wildlife. Some species of birds and mammals have been definitely threatened. Long term effects are still a mystery. However, most scientists working in the field take the position that while they do not know how bad a poison is for other animals (including man), no poison is likely to be good for you. Again the probability is that the skunks, for whom insects make up a major part of the diet, may be affected.

In the short term, say the rest of this century, my guess would be that the skunk probably will enter a declining cycle. In the long term, his chances of survival seem about as good as that of man, since he thrives in the same kind of environment. No one has any way of knowing how things will work out for either species, but whatever ultimately happens, it will probably happen for better or worse to men and skunks together.

The Marten

Several years ago I spent the spring and summer walking the length of the Appalachian Trail from Georgia to Maine. During the course of this two-thousand-mile hike I had a variety of encounters with wildlife (the expectation of such encounters was one of the reasons for making the long trip). The most unusual and memorable wildlife experience occurred in Maine, toward the end of the trail, and was a very brief one, lasting only a few seconds.

Late in the afternoon I was climbing up a steep mountainside, walking slowly, thinking about camp and how much heavier a pack is in the afternoon than it is in the morning. The trail was narrow, rough, slippery, and ascended the mountain in a series of sharp switchbacks. At one of these turns, the path skirted a large, flat boulder of exactly the right shape and size for leaning against, resting a pack upon. An important rule for all long distance hikers is: never pass up a good resting place; who knows when you will find another. Therefore, I sat down on the rock.

I had been there perhaps two or three minutes when I heard a sound a few yards below me on the mountain. I looked down in time to see a red squirrel leap from the trunk of one spruce tree to the ground, cross the trail I had just climbed, and with a desperate hop, scramble up, disappear into the top of another spruce on the far side of the trail. The squirrel was running fast and frantically. In less time than it has taken to write the last sentence, the reason for his speed and panic became obvious. The squirrel was running for his life, quite possibly making the last run of his life. Out of the spruce in hot pursuit came a marten, his tail stiff with excitement. The marten was across the path and up into the spruce even more swiftly than the terrified squirrel. I did not see or hear anything else of the chase, but the odds are that the marten won it, since there is no quicker mammal in the North American treetops and squirrels are a favorite prey of this agile hunter.

The Mustelidae family includes the three most specialized predatory mammals in North America. The digging badger, the swimming otter and the climbing marten. Though other predators, including members of the Mustelidae such as the weasels and fisher, sometimes hunt in the trees, no other North American mammal comes close to matching the marten's arboreal skill, and in fact, with the exception of the monkeys, few other animals anywhere are better, more agile climbers than the marten.

However, unlike the otter with his webbed feet, the badger with his powerful digging apparatus, the marten has not evolved dramatic adaptations that indicate his specialty and give him an obvious advantage in practicing it. The marten does have several physical characteristics which may be of service to him in his role as an arboreal hunter, but at best they are minor adaptations. His tail is relatively bushy, like that of a squirrel, and presumably it helps him maintain his balance as he leaps through the trees. However, it is no bushier than that of the skunk, who is no climber at all, the wolverine, who is only a fair climber, or the fisher, who, next to the marten, is the most arboreal of all the Mustelidae. The marten, unlike the other mustelids, has hair on the pads of his feet. This probably gives him a better grip as he speeds along branches. Also, in addition to the anal scent glands which are a common characteristic of most of the mustelids, the marten has a third, specialized gland. It is located near the center of his abdomen. When the marten moves along tree limbs, over stones or logs, the gland comes in contact with the surface and a faint scent trail is left behind. Presumably these scent trails help mark a marten's treetop territory for the benefit of others of his kind and serve as a method of attracting mates. It is a device which would be more necessary for an arboreal animal, whose trails and territory are located in the upper stories of the forest, than it would be for an animal traveling on the ground on more permanent paths.

Otherwise the marten is not equipped much differently than are the other mustelids of his size. He is a lithe, sinuous animal, somewhat larger than the mink. He hunts as the mink and weasels do, by pursuing his prey, catching it because of his superior speed and endurance. On the ground the marten's prey is similar to that of the smaller mustelids, consisting of rodents, ground birds, some reptiles and insects, carrion and occasionally some vegetable matter. In comparison with the otter or badger, the marten is a physically unspecialized specialist. He is simply a swift, agile animal who has taken to the trees. To a large extent the marten's specialty seems to rest on evolved habit, behavior, skill, rather than upon evolved physical adaptations.

Nevertheless, the marten is as much tied to his special environment, the deep evergreen forests of the north, as the otter is to the water or the badger to the loamy prairies. He is seldom found far

from this environment, and what happens to the forests determines, and apparently always has determined, what happens to the marten.

One important reason why the marten, though able to hunt on the ground, does not stray far from his special forest environment is the competition offered by other predators. On the ground the marten is only one among many medium-sized hunters—weasels, mink, skunks, foxes, cats. They may be no more efficient hunters than the marten but on the ground they are at least his peers, and he must compete with them for available prey on an equal basis. Above ground the situation is quite different—the marten has no equal. The marten does have competition in the trees—the fisher, smaller weasels, cats, occasional snakes, birds of prey are sometimes arboreal hunters—but the marten is obviously superior to them there as he is not on the ground.

There is another minor, somewhat related factor that tends to make the marten remain in the trees. As with all the Mustelidae, natural enemies, other predators preying on him, are not a serious threat to the marten. Being a quick, strong, well-armed animal, he does not make an easy catch. However, there are other hunters who can and sometimes will hunt marten on the ground—foxes, wolves, coyotes, bobcats, lynx, wolverines, fisher. However, with the possible and occasional exception of the semiarboreal fisher, none of these predators pose any threat to the marten in the trees. He is far too agile for them. Thus, not only is arboreal hunting less competitive for the marten, it is also somewhat less risky than ground hunting.

It is important to remember that the physical shape, special adaptations, behavior, range, specialty of a marten or any other animal is importantly influenced by other animals. This is particularly true of the predators whose relations with other animals are close and critical. Hunters are always in direct competition with other hunters and with their prey. In considering how animals influence each other, it is necessary to understand what biologists mean when they speak of an animal's "niche." A niche is partly a geographical area, the territory inhabited, but it is also the role an animal plays in the place he lives. Thus the otter's niche is that of a semiaquatic predator, the badger's that of a burrowing hunter. Sometimes a niche is determined by climate, for example that of the polar bear. The time of day may even determine the niche of a species. Thus red-tailed hawks and great horned owls often hunt the same geographical area but they occupy separate niches, the hawk's being daylight, while darkness belongs to the owl.

Each animal has his own niche, a role he performs at least somewhat more efficiently than any other creature in a given place. Though closely related animals, those with similar needs, often are extremely competitive, no two animals share exactly the same niche, or at least not for very long or harmoniously. Two different species trying to perform exactly the same role in exactly the same place would compete destructively. The importation of the mongoose to Jamaica is one of the rare examples of such a thing happening. The mongoose was equipped to take over the niches of the native island predators. Being so equipped, he did; being unable to occupy the same niche as the mongoose, the original hunters perished.

However, the importation of the mongoose was an accidental and most abnormal event. Generally what might be called the niche system works to avoid such fatal confrontations. Each species seeks (in an instinctive, evolutionary way) a niche where it will have a certain advantage over competing animals. All species seek to tighten their hold on their niche, defend it, and at the same time increase it by becoming more numerous, playing a larger role in a larger area. However, since each species is responding to similar evolutionary drives, all are pushing against each other, exerting pressure which prohibits any species from complete domination. Normally the advantage that any animal has over his competitors in playing a certain role in a certain place is a very slight one. Rarely is it large enough for him to completely eliminate a competitive species, conquer its niche. However, quite frequently this pressure, created by animals seeking to defend and expand niches, is sufficient to cause species to change their territory, change their habits, change their forms.

The ways in which animals act upon each other to bring about change are many, complex, subtle. However, with respect to the marten, there are two major factors producing this pressure to change. The marten is, in part, what he is today because of the nature of the animals on which he preys and the other predators who compete with him for that prey.

The explanation of how prey influences predators can perhaps be simplified by considering only the rodents who are the principal, though not exclusive quarry of the marten and other mustelids. At one time in the evolutionary past the ancestors of our rodents were all much alike, being small, perhaps ratlike creatures, rather unspecialized in comparison with their modern descendents. Partly to escape competition with their own kind for food and territory, partly to escape pressure from primitive predators, some of the rodents began to seek new niches, new roles, new territories, to specialize by changing their form and behavior. For example, some rodents evolved aquatic adaptations, habits, and in time became muskrats. Others took a different path, became climbers, became red squirrels. These changes put pressure on the predators. Obviously a hunter who could not climb had little chance of preying on a rodent who could. The marten, among others, chose (again this was an evolutionary, not willful, choice) not to let the primitive squirrels escape, and followed them into the trees, changing as the squirrels did, because they did. Other predators, the mink and otter for example, chose to pursue at evolutionary speed the rodents who were heading toward the water. In some ways the evolution of prey and predators might be compared to the development of military weapons in our age. When one nation develops a new weapon, other nations seek counterweapons to minimize the advantage of the first. So it is with species. When one ever so slowly changes its habits, develops a new specialty, it immediately puts pressure on many other species to make, so to speak, some countermove. The evolutionary movement is constant, changes are forever occurring; we are always in the process of becoming something else.

Just as the early rodents were all very similar animals so were the forerunners of the Mustelidae, probably being relatively unspecialized, weasel-like creatures. From that original stock, as we have seen, the various members of the family have come a long way in terms of variety and specialization. They changed—the marten became a marten, the mink a mink—because, as has been described, they were forced to change by their prey. But they also forced each other to change. The mink, in a certain sense, drove the marten into the trees, the marten pushed the mink toward the water. The primitive marten sought a new niche where he could escape competition with the primitive mink, sought a role in places where he had at least a slight advantage over the mink.

Though the marten and mink have diverged considerably, have occupied distinctive hunting niches, they are still to a degree competitive, still exert mutual pressure on each other, continue to force each other to become something else. To oversimplify somewhat, the marten, because of his adaptations, habits, has become the best red-squirrel hunter of all the Mustelidae, while the mink has specialized as a muskrat hunter. These two rodents are, in a sense, located in the heartland of the niches of the two mustelids. Despite specialization, a marten can and occasionally will prey on muskrats, sometimes finding an animal who has accidentally wandered or been driven upland. In the same way, a mink will sometimes catch a dull, weakened, disoriented red squirrel on the ground. However, this casual, accidental predation is a minor area of competition between the two hunters. The marten has no inclination and little ability to pursue a muskrat into the water. Once a red squirrel has escaped into the treetops he is safe from the mink.

However, there is another rodent (there are many but, to repeat, this is an oversimplified example), the snowshoe hare, who represents a dietary point of conflict between the two hunters. Not infrequently the marten comes down from the trees, the mink up from the wetlands, to hunt the hare. (Perhaps it would be more accurate to say that neither has as yet entirely abandoned his role as an upland hunter.) In doing so, both are hunting at the fringe of their niche, in a place and for prey where their advantage is much less than when they are in the treetops or marshes. Not only are the marten and mink perhaps a bit less efficient hare hunters than they are squirrel or muskrat killers, but also hare hunting is more competitive. The marten seldom if ever loses a squirrel in the trees to a mink, but on the ground he and the mink must contend for hares on more or less an equal basis. Also, as was described earlier in the chapter, both animals will be in direct competition with the predators who have remained upland hunters —the other mustelids and members of the cat and dog families.

In a figurative way, when the marten leaves the trees to hunt hares, he bumps into the mink and all the other ground hunters. His inclination is to bounce back into the trees where his advantage is greatest. Under normal circumstances the marten will concentrate on squirrel hunting, the mink on muskrats, picking up occasional easy hares as something of a predatory bonus. Only under abnormal conditions, when mink or martens become too abundant, when squirrels and muskrats become too scarce, will these hunters turn to the hare in earnest.

Seeking to survive in the easiest, safest way possible makes common, biological, evolutionary sense. All animals instinctively obey this logic. This seems to account for the fact that the direction of evolution is toward the development of more specialists. The drive of all species is to increase their advantage and build up the fortifications around their niche by developing additional adaptations. So far as is known, there are few, if any, examples of animals evolving toward a less specialized existence. In the same vein, the longer an order, class, phylum has been in existence, the more specialized it seems to become. For example, though the variety of mammals may seem remarkable, we are very much alike, none of us very specialized when compared with the insects who have had perhaps a half-billion years longer than we in which to seek solutions to the common problem of survival. With our accustomed arrogance we often think of the insects as being primitive, crude creatures. Actually they are, in evolutionary terms, not only much older, but often much more sophisticated than mammals. No mammals, including man, have, for example, developed such an ingenious social organization as that of the honeybee.

Though evolutionary changes are so slow as to be almost invisible, we sometimes observe phenomena that seem to illustrate the tendency of all living things to become more, rather than less, specialized. For example, the polar bear in ages past was a generalized bear, so to speak. At some point in the past he began to adapt as a specialized arctic hunter. The color of his coat changed so as to provide better camouflage in the land of perpetual snow. He became the best swimmer of all the bears so as to hunt large marine mammals. The process is still continuing. Studies of the polar bear indicate that he is becoming more and more aquatic both in habit and physical adaptations. It is predicted that if he survives long enough (this is unlikely, since the polar bear is now on the verge of extinction) he may become a sea bear similar in habits and adaptations to the sea lion.

There is a frequently observed characteristic of the marten which also seems to illustrate the pressure to specialize. In the beginning, when the ancestors of all the Mustelidae were less specialized than they are today, the likelihood is that all of them dealt with watery environments somewhat as does the modern weasel (who is probably similar to the ancestral mustelid). Though not an aquatic hunter, the weasel has no particular dislike of water, hunts occasionally in the wetlands, swims when necessary. From this point of departure, the otter, and to a lesser extent the mink, became aquatic specialists, while most other members of the family remained at least water-tolerant. The marten, however, having moved in a different direction, toward the trees, is the exception. Today he is not only the least water-loving of the Mustelidae but actually seems to loathe the element.

Being a northern creature, the marten is hardly delicate and is quite able to withstand the long, semiarctic winters without hibernating. However, unlike the other weasels, getting wet is a hardship that the marten will go to great lengths to avoid. The marten never gets wet if he can help it, denning up not when it is cold but when it is wet. He takes no aquatic prey and the prospect of crossing a brook or pond, which another mustelid would ford without a second thought, seems to panic a marten. He has been observed traveling along such water barriers apparently looking for a fallen tree that may serve as a bridge, or a raft of driftwood on which he can ride, and stay dry.

The marten's dislike of water is probably partly a matter of habit, psychology. Having become an arboreal specialist, he seldom encounters this element, which, being strange, may well frighten him now. However, he is not inclined to get wet for physical reasons as well. Unlike many of the other mustelids, the marten's coat does not shed water easily. If he is doused, his fur rapidly becomes and remains heavy, sodden with water, a great handicap for an animal that depends upon being able to leap through the trees. Also, though I know of no studies of the subject, it is quite possible that the marten, no longer accustomed to water, may be less resistant to water chill than the other mustelids, less immune to respiratory diseases associated with this condition.

The marten's dislike of and inability to cope with water indicates how far he has diverged from the other mustelids and the probable direction of his specialization. His future seems to be in the trees and the chances are he will, if allowed sufficient time, become more arboreal than he is now. Already the marten does most of his traveling above ground, sometimes going several miles without touching foot on the ground. Also the marten is devoted to sun bathing, sprawling out on a limb to soak in light and warmth.

These habits the marten shares with other tree-loving animals, including the monkeys, who, in time, he will probably more closely resemble than he does now.

Up to this point, using the marten as an example, we have considered the advantages of specialization. In general, the advantage is that the more specialized an animal becomes, the better able he is to perform a specific role in a specific place, and the greater is his advantage over less specialized competitors. However, there are grave risks to specialization, and again the marten illustrates the situation.

In the first place, when an animal specializes, evolves new behavior, skills, a new form, he inevitably loses something. Thus the marten, in becoming an arboreal hunter, has lost much of the ability and inclination to deal with water that other mustelids possess. He can do some things now that he could not do in a more primitive form, but there are things that he can't (or won't) do now that he once could. An even more dramatic example of this is the sea otter. This hunter too probably began as a relatively unspecialized weasel-like animal. Now he is entirely aquatic. Not only is he unable to climb a tree or chase a rabbit, he is virtually helpless on land, which was once his domain.

Specialization tends to create for the animal a sort of biological cage, imprisoning him in his special niche. The more he specializes the smaller and stronger this cage becomes. To put it another way, the farther an animal goes down one specialized evolutionary path, the fewer his biological alternatives are, the less flexible his response to pressure from his environment and other creatures. As long as the environment in which the animal specializes remains in good working order, the animal is in an advantageous position. However if that environment is altered the specialist animal is put at a great disadvantage. The more specialized an animal becomes, the more vulnerable he is to change in his environment. This is a great risk, because as the past history of the world indicates, environmental changes (great shifts in temperature, terrain, precipitation) occur much more rapidly than evolutionary changes. It takes a long time to make a specialist, an equally long time to unmake him and make him into another kind. Usually species are not given this time (the dinosaur being a prime example). A specialist who becomes obsolete due to sudden environmental changes usually perishes before he becomes something else.

The marten again illustrates this point. He is superbly adapted to hunting in thick interlocking evergreen forests. Two centuries ago when this sort of forest covered much of the northern United States and southern Canada, the marten, by all accounts (the best being the records kept by early fur buyers), was a relatively common animal. Now, however, he is one of the rarest predators in the United States, much less common than he formerly was in Canada and Alaska. There are various reasons for his decline (some of which will be discussed later) but an obvious one is that millions of acres of evergreen forest have been cut for timber, cleared for agricultural land. There was a very quick (in evolutionary terms), massive change and reduction in the marten's special environment.

All animals have become specialized to a degree. As an obvious example, life on earth began in the seas. The basic specialization of terrestrial creatures is that we left the water, became adapted to living on land, breathing the air (naturally we gave up something—our ability to live and breathe in the water). However, the degree of specialization varies considerably between species, families, orders of animals. By accident or in obedience to natural laws which we do not understand, some animals seem, in an evolutionary way, to have dragged their feet in this matter of specialization, to have refused opportunities to become specially adapted to special niches, to have stubbornly remained what might be called generalists, biological jacks-of-many-trades.

We know so little of the origin and development of animals that it is very dangerous to make sweeping judgments about the success or failure of evolutionary experiments; for example, trying to judge between the generalist and specialist. In the short run (and we are thinking in terms of thousands of years), there is great pressure on every animal to specialize; and in the short run, animals that do specialize, seek specific niches, may have considerable success. However, in the very long run, the generalists, the animals which for some reasons have been more resistant to this pressure, seem to be the most enduring and successful. The reason appears to be, as mentioned above, that the more specialized an animal becomes, the more vulnerable he is to change.

The natural history of this continent during the past two hundred years serves among other things as an example of what happens to animals who must deal with rapid environmental changes. In almost every instance the generalist animals have come through the period of change, are dealing with the changes, more successfully than the specialists. The bass has done better than the trout, the garter snake than the rattler, red-tailed hawk than the peregrine, rat than the prairie dog, coyote than the wolf.

Then, of course, there is the evidence of our own species. We men are among the least specialized of all mammals. In comparison with the others, we do not run, swim, fly, climb, dig, see, hear, smell, fight exceptionally well. However, we do many of these things moderately well. We have remained physical generalists, inhabiting, though often precariously, an immensely broad niche. Our one specialty has been our ability to generalize—in other words, to think and abstract. After perhaps a quarter of a million years, in competition with what would appear to be much better equipped specialists, we generalists have come to the place where we are supreme. What comes next, whether or not, as some think, we may have now started down the dangerous evolutionary road of specialization, remains to be seen.

Among the North American predators the recent history of the Mustelidae serves as a very neat illustration of this specialist *versus* generalist matter. Prior to the great environmental upheavals caused by the invasion of the continent by European man, the six most common mustelids in what is now the continental United States were the otter, badger, marten, mink, skunk, and weasel. The first three were more specialized predators than the latter three. Pre-European natural-history records are scanty, but such as they are, they indicate that in terms of range and numbers the three specialists were at least as successful as the generalists. Then, from the standpoint of the wildlife, came the deluge—the continent-altering Europeans. Today the three specialized hunters are extinct in many parts of their former range, uncommon everywhere. The three generalists appear to be at least holding their own and in some cases are more widely distributed, more numerous than they were in the pre-European days.

The weasel, mink, skunk in the pre-European days were accustomed to living, breeding, hunting in various territories—the forest, scrubby thickets, meadows, bottomlands, in the north, south, along the seacoast, in the mountains. When the changes came, when the Europeans began turning forests into meadows, meadows into farms, farms into suburbs, the three generalized mustelids did not suffer greatly. They found in the new environment features which approximated the old, and from their standpoint some that were an improvement. (For example, the garbage can, a device unknown previously on this continent, has been a boon to the skunk.) Having hunted in many ways and places for a variety of prey, the three generalists were able to relate and adapt their old habits and needs to the new environment.

With the marten and the other specialists it was much different. The marten's prey, his security, his whole style of life was closely associated with the heavy, continuous evergreen forests. There was little place in the new environment for him to play his tradi-

tional role. In some ways when the forests disappeared, were reduced, the marten was in the same position that the blacksmiths
were when the automobile replaced the horse. Both had skills they
could not use—both were, in a sense, obsolete.

This, of course, raises an obvious question. If a blacksmith can,
as many did, switch over to a new trade, become an auto mechanic,
for example, why cannot the marten do likewise and develop new
skills more suitable for the changed environment? The question
seems more pertinent with regard to the marten than, say, the
otter or badger, since the latter two animals have gone farther
down the path of specialization and evolved physiques that obviously tie them to specific environments—the water, the diggable
earth. The marten had few such adaptations. In his forest territory
the marten is quite capable of hunting the same upland creatures
as the mink, weasel, or skunk. Why, when the forests fell, did
not the marten begin hunting mice in wheatfields, rats under
barns, garbage in the suburbs?

The answer is, of course, that the skills of a blacksmith are
learned during the course of a few years. The habits, responses,
adaptations of the marten *evolved* during the course of thousands
of years; they were not learned and therefore cannot be unlearned.
As for the skunk, mink, weasel, because they were generalists
some of their evolved skills and habits were applicable to the post-
European environment of this continent, while the specialist was
unable to cope with anything but his traditional forest.

It is easy to observe physical specialization in animals, webbed
feet for example, and the risks of such adaptations are obvious.
What might be called psychological specialization, innate behavior
patterns, are less obvious but no less important in terms of specialization, as the marten illustrates. For example, some of the best

places in the United States to see martens are in our large western parks, such as Yellowstone and Yosemite. Here, where the forest remains more or less intact, the marten is relatively common. In the parks, martens often are seen around picnic and camping areas looking for food, and have become fairly regular and adept garbage-can robbers. This behavior suggests that the marten is intelligent enough, and physically able, to survive in many of the same places, in much the same way, as do skunks, mink, and weasels. However, the fact remains that the marten does not, will not, leave his traditional forest niche. Since it is impossible to psychoanalyze a marten, any answer to the puzzle amounts to pure speculation. However, I have the feeling that the marten does not leave the backwoods for the same reason some human hermits will not. They have spent their lives in the boondocks, like it there, and are shy about trying to cope with a strange environment.

While the marten does seem to be a good example of the predatory specialist and of the evolutionary risks of specialization, it should be repeated and re-emphasized that the condition of any animal is determined by any number of subtle interrelated factors, never by just one. For example, while it seems true that the marten has been figuratively trapped by his specialty, that he has declined because the forests where he specializes have declined, he has also been literally trapped with steel. He probably would have declined after the coming of the Europeans even if the forests had remained untouched. Like all the mustelids, the marten has been trapped for his fur, but the marten has been under special pressure from trappers. His fur has always been of great value. In Europe the marten is known as the sable, and sable is, of course, the fur from which some of the most expensive regal garments are made. When it was discovered that the sable also inhabited North America, this valuable fur not only became a prize for trappers, but getting fur became a motive for exploration, conquest, commercial expansion in the north. Not only was (and is) the marten one of the most valuable furbearers (a single skin may sell for fifty to a hundred dollars) but he is one of the easiest to trap. Like all the mustelids, the marten is very curious, and perhaps because as an arboreal hunter he naturally has so few things he need fear, the marten is even more innocent about traps than the other members of his family. Any sort of bait, almost any sort of trap, will take a marten. Often trappers did not even bother with packing in heavy steel traps for martens. They simply set up crude deadfall arrangements which could be made in a few minutes out of material at hand.

In the early days of the fur trade, records of fur-buying companies showed that as many as thirty or forty thousand American sable pelts would be marketed each year. Now the figure is less than ten thousand, almost all of which come from Canada or Alaska, where less alteration has occurred in the favored environment of this animal. Today only a few hundred marten pelts a year are taken in the continental United States, and in many of the states the marten has been given a protected legal status. Also, as has been the case with other members of the Mustelidae whose fur is valuable, and as a result are becoming rare, efforts are being made to raise the marten in captivity. The United States Fish and Wildlife Service has had some success experimenting with marten ranches. Considering the growing scarcity of these animals it seems almost certain that if sable is to be used by the fur trade in the future, the pelts will largely be supplied by breeders rather than trappers.

The Fisher

Popular names for animals often leave something to be desired
when it comes to accuracy. Vampire bats, chicken hawks, and sea
lions are examples of animals whose names are misleading, to say
the least. In this category must be included the fisher cat, the common name of a relatively uncommon, large, northern mustelid.
The fisher is obviously not a cat, no more than any of the family
is, and does not resemble one, looking like what he is—a very
large marten. Nor is this cat a fisher. He is often found around
water in swampy country and preys on some aquatic animals. He
may occasionally be able to pull a live fish from the shallows, and
frequently will feed on dead fish he finds along the shore, but he
is not a fisher in the sense that the mink or the otter is. (Fisher
would have been a particularly descriptive name for the otter.)

If it seemed necessary to name this animal after two other animals, mink-marten, or something of that nature, would have been
more suitable. The misnamed fisher resembles these smaller
mustelids both in appearance and habit. As the family is classified
by zoologists, the fisher is most closely related to the marten, be-
longing to the same genus, and is sometimes called in natural-

history guides the Pennant's marten (after an early naturalist). Like his smaller cousin, the marten, the fisher is a richly furred, bushy-tailed animal. Also, he is a good climber, next to the marten the most accomplished mustelid in the trees. However, quite unlike the marten, who detests water, the fisher is fond of wetlands, and hunts them after the fashion of the mink.

In the preceding chapter the mink and marten were discussed in terms of the separate niches that they occupy. On the face of it, the fisher, who hunts in much the same way, often in the same places as the mink and marten, would seem to contradict the theory that each animal has a niche that he and he alone occupies. It is true that the fisher is a competitor of the two smaller mustelids (as, of course, are many other hunters—cats, dogs, otters, weasels, wolverines) and that he is often found in the same territory as the mink and the marten. However, he plays a somewhat different role, exerts a different pressure in the prey-predator relationships than they do, and thus occupies a niche of his own.

Perhaps the easiest way to explain the difference between the niche of the fisher and his two smaller relatives is to say that he fills the role of a large hunter in the trees and wetlands, while theirs is that of a small or medium-sized hunter. In the previous chapter it was noted that factors other than geography and topography often determine an animal's niche. The example was given of the red-tailed hawk and great horned owl, who share the same range, hunt much the same prey. The niches of these two birds are separated by light—the hawk is a daylight hunter, the owl a bird of the darker hours. In the same way, size can create an animal's niche, separate it from that of competing creatures.

The fisher weighs from twelve to twenty pounds, often ten times as much as a mink or marten. In a sense, becoming larger has been the evolutionary move of the fisher, his specialty, the direction he has moved to escape direct competition with other mustelids and predators. Because of his greater size the fisher can do some things that the mink and marten cannot do, and at the same time, since there is always some penalty for specialization, his bulk prohibits him from doing some of the things they can do.

For example, the fisher is a good climber, good enough to be able occasionally to catch and kill his smaller relative, the marten. However, this is a relatively rare occurrence. Not only is the marten more agile (in part because he is smaller) but if pursued by a fisher, normally has a certain sanctuary. A three-pound marten can go up and out in trees until he comes to limbs so small that they simply will not bear the weight of a fifteen-pound fisher no matter how agile he may be. For the same reason, the fisher may sometimes prey on red squirrels, but his great bulk makes it impossible for him to pursue these animals in the same places and in the same way, with the same efficiency as the marten.

A similar situation exists with regard to the mink. A fisher hunting in a swamp, on the edges of a lake or stream, may sometimes catch a mink, but normally a mink can retreat to the deeper water where, being smaller and a better swimmer, his chances of escape will be good. Also, when hunting the wetlands, a fisher will prey on the same quarry that a mink does, muskrats for example, but he is not quite as good at this sort of hunting as the more aquatic mink.

One obvious way in which size determines the role, and thus the niche, of any predator is in the kind of animals on which he can prey. Large hunters, while they may often feed on relatively small game, have, because of great strength and bulk, the option of hunting bigger game. This is the case of the fisher in comparison

with smaller members of the Mustelidae. In the uplands of the northern evergreen forests, the fisher, like many other predators, often preys on the snowshoe hare. The hare, other small rodents such as chipmunks, voles, mice, along with small semiaquatic reptiles, probably in normal times make up the bulk of the fisher's diet. However, the fisher can hunt other animals, prey which is simply too large for the smaller upland predators. The fisher, for example, has been known to prey upon both foxes and bobcats. Even more surprisingly, there is good evidence that the fisher successfully hunts deer.

One memorable winter morning in the western Maine wilderness, I had a chance to discuss this matter—how any fifteen-pound animal, even one of the strong, quick mustelids, can bring down a hundred-pound deer—with a friend who is one of the most knowledgeable field naturalists of the north that I know. His name is Jim Drake and for nearly thirty years he has lived in the Maine woods, supporting himself as a lumberjack, surveyor, trapper, guide, so as to remain close to, continue to learn about the wildlife of the area. Unlike many so-called woodsmen, whose only real curiosity about an animal is whether it is best to hook it or shoot it, Jim is a true naturalist, curious about all manner of creatures and their relationships with one another.

The morning in question was a cold, bright one. The temperature was well below zero when we set out with a snow sled and snowshoes from Jim's lakeside cabin. During the night two or three inches of new snow had fallen on three or four feet of old snow. In theory, the reason we were out was to visit a mountain pond where Jim had set some beaver traps. However, both of us were less interested in dead beavers than we were in meandering through the woods, reading signs in the new snow, finding out who had been doing what during the previous night.

Among other animals who had been moving during the night were at least two fishers. The fisher leaves a distinctive trail, if not a track, as he bounds along through the woods, leaping three or four feet at a time. At the end of each bound the animal slides, and in loose snow, such as we had that morning, the paw mark is often smudged. After a time, when wind, drifting, melting have obliterated parts of the trail, an individual fisher print can be confusing, mistaken for a fox or bobcat. However on this morning the fisher trails were fresh and easy to follow. There seemed to be no particular pattern to the fisher's travels. Like the other mustelids, these animals hunt by simply crisscrossing their range until they come across fresh signs or the maker of the signs. We followed one of the fishers, a large male, Jim estimated from the tracks, for a half hour or so. He had come down an old logging road, then veered off into a tangled ravine through which flowed a small stream. The fisher had stopped several times to investigate old stumps, poke under fallen logs and into dense bushes, presumably looking for mice, rabbits, or grouse. At one point he came across a deer trail, turned and followed it, which brought up the subject of the fisher as a deer killer.

Not a few woodsmen tend to pass along hearsay, rumor, and myth as fact but Jim is a very cautious natural historian. He said that he had never personally seen a fisher kill a deer. However, he had observed fishers feeding on deer carcasses, and seen signs that seemed to indicate fisher had been running deer. Finally, he had talked to others, whose observations were usually reliable, who had seen these hunters killing deer. He therefore tended to go along with the common belief that the fisher does prey on deer. Talking it over as we slogged along on snowshoes, it seemed to us that predation of this kind probably took place under fairly special circumstances—during the winter when all hunters are forced to take whatever game they can, and in the deep snow when the fisher, who can move over the tops of the drifts, would have a considerable advantage over the deer, who must break through them. By piecing together what we had both seen and heard from others, it seemed reasonable that whatever deer a fisher does take were very likely late fawns from the spring or old, feeble, crippled animals. Deer would be marginal prey for the fisher, and deer taken by fishers would be marginal animals, those of least biological value to the herd as a whole. As to how a fisher could kill even a weakened deer, two hunting techniques, both reflecting the special faculties of the fisher, may be involved. Like all the mustelids, the fisher, though not particularly swift in terms of straightaway speed, is very quick and enduring. In the snow this hunter could stay on the fresh trail of deer until he so exhausted and confused his prey as to be able to catch him. Jim had also heard that fisher, being good climbers, would lay in wait on the branch of a tree over a deer trail and drop on their prey from above.

While deer are only occasional prey of the fisher, the fact that the fisher may, under special circumstances, take deer, sets him aside from, gives him a special niche as compared to, the smaller mustelids—mink, marten, weasels—who, hunting in the uplands, cannot prey upon deer under any circumstances. In the other territories, wetlands and trees, where the fisher moves into what might be thought of as the special preserve of the mink and marten, the same situation holds true. Because of his size he can prey on creatures who seldom, if ever, are hunted by his smaller relatives. In the wetlands, while he and the mink may compete directly for muskrats (with the more agile aquatic mink probably being more efficient), the fisher can also take an occasional beaver, which because of its great size is seldom preyed upon by the mink.

It is, however, in the trees that the fisher has become most famous as a specialized hunter. He may take a few squirrels but, as has been noted, he is too heavy to pursue these animals very far or high into the treetops. However, there is another arboreal rodent in the northern forests which the fisher is quite capable of catching and has made a specialty of killing. This is the porcupine, which is a staple of the fisher's diet, just as the muskrat is for the mink, the red squirrel for the marten.

Along with the skunk, the porcupine has evolved the most unusual and effective defensive weapon on any North American mammal. As with the skunk, the porcupine is generally avoided by predators because it is painful to do otherwise. In times of hardship some of the hunting mammals will prey on porcupines, but when they do, they run a considerable risk. More than one member of the dog, cat, even bear family has died because of porcupine quills, which may cause festering wounds or, if swallowed, puncture vital internal organs.

The fisher, however, has learned to take advantage of what is literally a chink in the porcupine's formidable armor. There are no quills on the porcupine's stomach, and the fisher, finding the animal on the ground or driving him down from the trees, simply flips him on his back, taking care to avoid the thrashing, quill-studded tail as he does so. Once so exposed, the otherwise defenseless porcupine is easily dispatched.

The fisher's known preference for porcupines, his skill as a porcupine hunter, has been the basis for a curious partnership with man, one which was established because men have come to recognize the constructive role of predation. Throughout the northern part of the country where timber is an important natural resource and lumbering a major industry, the porcupine is regarded as a great pest. Moving slowly, methodically, from tree to tree, porcupines feed on the bark, girdle the trunk, kill or weaken (by making them vulnerable to disease) many trees.

The amount of timber ruined by porcupines may not be as great as lumbermen often claim, but still there is some loss, and it is the kind of loss calculated to enrage men. For years porcupine bounties have been paid by some states where lumbering is an important industry. In addition, state agents and private timbermen have made periodic efforts to eliminate porcupines by poisoning or shooting them. However, these methods have proved to be time-consuming, expensive, and not as effective as loggers had hoped they would be. In many areas, despite various efforts to control them, porcupines have continued to gnaw away on usable timber, even become more abundant than they formerly were.

About five years ago, biologists attached to the United States Forest Service recognized that the porcupine problem was becoming more serious because the porcupine's natural enemies, chiefly the fisher, had been largely eliminated from the forests. One obvious answer to the problem was to try to bring back the fisher. To accomplish this, the Forest Service (and, later, private lumber companies) began to buy live fishers trapped in Canada where the animal is still relatively common. These were shipped to the United States and released in selected forest areas in Wisconsin, Michigan, Colorado, Oregon, upper New England. As yet, not enough time has elapsed to determine the results of the experiment. However, there is some evidence that the reintroduction of the fisher has tended to reduce the number of porcupines.

Some fifteen years ago I hiked through the New England mountains. At that time porcupines were everywhere, particularly about camps. They were so numerous that at night it became a matter of routine to hang your pack by a string, in such a way that the porcupines could not reach it. (Porcupines crave salt. A sweaty pack strap, canoe paddle, pair of shoes, or a food pack is a great delicacy for them. If given a chance they will get the salt by gnawing these items.) Some nights we would throw salt on the ground around the camp, then sit back watching and listening to the porcupines who would congregate, snuffling and chomping away like so many small pigs. On this first trip through New England, while porcupines were very common, the fisher was regarded as rare, if not extinct, in the area.

Two years ago I hiked again through New England, from Mount Katahdin in Maine to the Green Mountains of Vermont. During the trip I saw only one porcupine. However, many trappers and hunters I talked to said that they now encountered fishers and fisher signs frequently. The experience of my friend, Jim Drake, in western Maine has been similar. Hedgehogs, as porcupines are called in that country, have become scarce, while, as recounted earlier, there were at least enough fishers in the area for Jim and me to find the trails of two animals in one morning.

The willingness of the Forest Service and other public and private agencies to try to control porcupines biologically by re-introducing the fisher is a hopeful sign, indicating a more sophisticated approach to wildlife management. Not only does such a program re-establish an interesting animal, it shows an awareness of the dangers involved in artificial controls, poisoning, bounty payments.

The relationship between the fisher and his favorite prey, the porcupine, illustrates the useful nature of predation, useful not only for the wild species involved but for man as well. The fisher and other wild porcupine hunters became scarce or extinct in the northern forests largely because of man. The fisher, for example, has declined for much the same reason that the marten has. First the forest environment was reduced and altered. The fisher, like the marten, is a hunter that apparently cannot or will not adapt easily to new types of environment. Secondly, like most of the Mustelidae, the fisher is a valuable and easily trapped furbearer. (At times in the past a single prime fisher pelt might have brought over a hundred dollars.)

However, in this matter it is quite pointless to wring our hands about the ignorance and greed of our ancestors. They were probably no worse than we are in the greedy use of our natural resources, and so far as their ignorance is concerned they had the excuse that no one, including early biologists, understood as well as we do today the nature of the delicate balance between wild species, the constructive role of predation.

We, on the other hand, have learned of these things, not only through the studies of biologists but by bitter experience. What happened between the fisher and porcupine in the northern forests, between deer, wolves, mountain lions in the Kaibab Plateau, are dramatic examples of how men, as well as wild species, benefit from the normal relationship between prey and predators. There are many equally important, if more commonplace, examples of the same phenomenon. In Yellowstone Park, for example, there are so many elk that they are ruining their range, and rangers must spend part of each fall slaughtering the excess animals so as to protect the elk from the elk. In South Dakota there are too many foxes (largely because too many coyotes have been shot or poisoned). In the past few years foxes have drastically reduced the pheasant population of that state, and pheasant hunting has been an important source of income for many South Dakota residents.

In Michigan, Pennsylvania, New York and other states, we have too many deer. Each year the animals cause substantial agricultural losses. To support the herd for sport hunters, state agencies must undertake expensive, time-consuming, artificial feeding programs. Despite such efforts, deer in these overpopulated areas are becoming less attractive to deer hunters (as opposed to deer killers). As it did in the Kaibab Forest, the fierce deer-against-deer competition tends to produce herds in which individual animals are smaller, weaker, less alert than they are where the overpopulation problem is not severe. Finally, throughout the country the depredations of numerous small rodents, mice, rats, voles, and certain insects are a continuing, often increasing problem. The economic loss they cause is the immediate concern of farmers, businessmen, homeowners, who suffer it, but these animals and our efforts to control them artificially may present a much more serious long-range problem. Each year we dump more and more poison—powders, dusts, sprays—into our environment as we attempt to cope with these pests. No one is quite sure what the ultimate effects of this vast poisoning program will be (and this ignorance is one of the most frightening aspects of it), but few scientists believe that we are improving the environment for ourselves or any other species.

The elimination of predators, the shattering of ancient relationships between the hunters and hunted have contributed greatly to many of the present biological, environmental crises. Thus the experiment with the fisher in the northern forests, an experiment aimed at re-establishing one of the relationships, re-introducing a biological control, is viewed as an important one by many biologists and conservationists. However, interesting as it may be, it would be misleading to suggest that biological controls—re-establishing predators—can be a practical solution for many of the major wildlife crises. For example, lions, bears, wolves once hunted in Pennsylvania, and when they did, partly because they did, there was no problem of too many deer such as that state has now. But too much time has passed, we men have brought about too many changes for anyone to suggest seriously that we could solve the Pennsylvania deer problem by importing lions, bears, and wolves in quantity. The big predators would survive for only a few hunting seasons. While they did, they would be a nuisance, perhaps even a menace. Because the environment has been so radically altered they probably would not perform an effective role in controlling deer.

We can't return to the old (pre-European) self-adjusting natural system, attractive as it may seem. The environmental, biological problems that we face are of our own making, and we must deal with them consciously, using human intelligence and ingenuity. In facing them we should realize that whatever we can do to preserve at least remnants of the original natural system, for example, prey-predator relationships, will be to our benefit.

The Wolverine

For centuries the wolverine has been regarded with a mixture of awe, superstition, fear; thought to be an animal of unnatural cunning, ferocity, maliciousness. To a greater extent than any of our other native animals the wolverine has played the role of a sort of home-grown monster, serving, at least for storytelling, as the North American version of a mythical griffin or dragon. Though it is now generally, if a bit reluctantly, recognized that the wolverine is a large, powerful, rare mammal rather than a heraldic beast, our understanding of this animal is confused by the legends, tall tales, horror stories that were so long associated with him. Even now it sometimes develops that what we have thought were wolverine facts turn out to be only imaginative wolverine fictions. Therefore, when describing the animal, it is well to be conservative so as to avoid unintentionally spreading the legends. However, even excessive caution does not obscure the fact that the wolverine is a remarkable animal.

The obvious characteristics which set the wolverine apart from the other mustelids are his size and strength. Weighing up to fifty pounds, the wolverine is much the largest of the land-going mustelids (the seal-like sea otter is somewhat larger) and, after the bear, wolf and puma, is the biggest of the North American predators. The wolverine is a chunky, stout-bodied, short-legged animal, in conformation somewhat resembling a small bear. Even among the weasels, who are particularly muscular animals, the wolverine is an animal of extraordinary strength, very likely one of the strongest animals in the world, pound for pound, and stronger than many animals who are many times his size.

There are so many stories told about the strength of the wolverine that it is difficult to sift fact from fiction. Among the commonest are accounts of trapped wolverines traveling miles through the deep snow with trap and attached log weighing fifty, one hundred, two hundred pounds, two tons, dragging along behind. However, one well-documented observation was made by naturalists on Mt. McKinley in Alaska. A wolverine killed a Dall sheep, weighing about one hundred and fifty pounds, on a mountain ridge. The wolverine carried the sheep for a mile and a half, through the snow, down the mountain, across a river and up a steep riverbank before finding a place to commence feeding. This is roughly the equivalent of a man carrying a seven-hundred-and-fifty-pound weight across similar terrain.

Unlike the other stout-bodied mustelids, the skunk and badger, which are relatively slow-moving animals, the wolverine has not sacrificed speed for strength. Though not as quick and agile as the weasel or mink, the wolverine is a speedy and remarkably enduring runner. Moving at the humpbacked lope typical of the family, wolverines can run down a deer or moose, and have been known to run away from wolves. Also, more like the small weasels than the heavy badgers and skunk, the wolverine is hyperactive, constantly on the move crisscrossing his hunting territory on the lookout for food or food signs. However, again in keeping with his reputation, the range of the wolverine is immense. Whereas the weasel may roam over a mile or two, the wolverine may travel a hundred miles or so to patrol his hunting territory. In the arctic wilderness wolverines seem to follow definite hunting trails, wide paths which often parallel game traces. Usually the wolverine's hunting route comprises an enormous, rough circle and it may take the animal a week or two to make a complete circuit of his range.

While he is active after the fashion of the small weasels, the wolverine, being stout-bodied, does carry fat on his frame and therefore, when hunting is hard, he can fast, utilizing stored energy, as the small slim members of the Mustelidae cannot. However, unlike the stout-bodied skunk and badger, the wolverine seldom dens up, sleeps through bad weather, even though he ranges through arctic and subarctic regions where the weather is ferocious.

In other respects the wolverine is something of a composite mustelid, possessing certain of the special characteristics and adaptations which have evolved in other individuals of the family. For example, next to the badger and skunk, the wolverine is the most accomplished digger among the mustelids. He has powerful shoulders, well-developed foreclaws. Like the badger he is quite capable of digging out a ground squirrel, ripping apart a log in search of grubs, rearranging a rock pile while hunting for a hare. However, the wolverine is also capable of catching a hare in open chase, as the badger is not.

The wolverine is sometimes called skunk bear, which rightly suggests that he is an odoriferous animal. Though he cannot spray musk as his smaller relative does, the wolverine produces it

in quantity and of a quality which is no less repellant than the glandular secretion of the skunk. However, the wolverine's scent-producing capacity does not serve as a prime defensive weapon as does the skunk's. The wolverine is such a strong, quick, formidable animal that few other hunters will molest him no matter how he smells. The wolverine's musk does serve to protect his belongings, if not his person. Like some other members of his family, the wolverine eats carrion and also has the habit of caching excess food, hiding it under brush, snow, the earth, returning to feed at a later time. Frequently the wolverine will douse such a store with his musk, thus making the meat unpalatable to, protecting it from, other foraging carnivores.

Though not specially adapted to the water as is the otter, nor as water-loving as the mink, the wolverine is a strong swimmer, quite capable of crossing lakes and rivers in search of prey, often hunting for aquatic creatures, birds, mammals, reptiles in shallow water. Finally, though a large, stocky animal, the wolverine is a good climber, not as agile as the marten but sufficiently so to scramble into the top branches of a tree if the need arises.

Given his adaptations and faculties, the wolverine is able to prey on virtually all of the animals that are hunted by his lesser relatives, from grubs to rodents and birds, with mice, lemmings, grouse, hares apparently making up the bulk of his diet. In addition, because of his greater size and strength the wolverine can, and sometimes does, take prey far too large to be managed by the lesser mustelids. Deer, moose, elk, sheep all are sometimes killed by the wolverine. Sometimes it appears from signs that the wolverine makes use of his climbing ability to bring down such big game, waiting on a branch above a game trail, dropping down on the animal's back. When it comes to what the wolverine can kill, will

140

eat, it is probably safe to assume that there is scarcely any prey species within his range that he cannot kill, will not eat, under the proper circumstances.

Some of the most fantastic wolverine stories have to do with his relations with other large predators. Like all members of the Mustelidae, the wolverine is an aggressive animal, rather excitable, quite ready to defend himself and his belongings. However, unlike the tiny weasel, the wolverine has the bulk and strength to back up his temper. There are reliable reports of a wolverine chasing away from his own kill (or from theirs) much larger predators—coyotes, wolves, mountain lions, even a pair of black bears. There is at least one apparently authentic report of a wolverine killing a mountain lion. The carcass of the lion and the signs of the struggle left no doubt that the cat was alive when the wolverine attacked. However, there is no way to tell the condition of the lion initially—it may have been weakened, crippled or wounded. While such incidents do occur, they most certainly do not occur as often as tellers of wolverine tall tales would have one believe. In the first place, wolverines and other large predators will not meet frequently. Secondly, like all wild hunters, it is to the wolverine's advantage, and it is his inclination, to survive as easily as he can, taking as few risks as necessary. He will not habitually make a practice of confronting, much less attacking, large, dangerous animals, no more than they will be inclined to confront him. Though they are not as well publicized, perhaps because they tend to deflate the mythical reputation of the wolverine, there are also records of bears and wolves chasing wolverines away from their kill and also several accounts of hungry wolves hunting down wolverines.

While it is a habit of men to seek out other animals, challenge them for the purpose of proving how tough and dangerous they are, establishing their manhood, this is not a type of behavior observed in other species. Wild predators apparently have no psychological need to challenge their peers. Wolverines, wolves, bears, big cats normally avoid each other because it makes no biological sense to do otherwise. However, it is accurate to say that, though the smallest of the large northern predators, the wolverine is so formidable as to have virtually no natural enemies except man. Only under rare circumstances would an adult wolverine be endangered by another wild hunter.

Given the wolverine's nature and behavior, which even unadorned by exaggeration are extraordinary, plus the fact that he is a wide-ranging, relatively uncommon inhabitant of the wild, lonely, empty north, it is not really surprising that he should have become the object of myths and legends. Almost invariably the gist of these wolverine stories has been that the animal is a mysterious, malicious, magical demon.

As an example of how these myths grew: From the fact that wolverines will sometimes chase bears and wolves away from their kill—and ignoring equally true reports that wolverines are sometimes the pursued rather than the pursuers—came the notion that wolverines regularly prey upon these large carnivores, who are terrified of the wolverine. Some Indians of the Canadian Northwest firmly believe that if a wolverine appears in a territory all other big hunters will immediately vacate it out of fear.

Another kind of story grew out of the experience of trappers. The wolverine, like other predators, tends to be curious, because curiosity is a useful trait in a hunter. There are true stories about wolverines following trappers as they put out a line of sets, tearing apart the traps, stealing bait or trapped furbearers. Such behavior is not surprising, since a wolverine could be expected to learn quickly that a man traveling through the woods is likely to flush game or leave food behind him. However, from these incidents has grown the myth, still current in the north, that the wolverine is a man hunter, a man killer. If, of course, one can believe that wolverines regularly kill bears and wolves, then it is not hard to believe that a wolverine trailing a trapper is not looking for food scraps but for the man himself. Several years ago I spent part of the spring and early summer in the western Canadian Arctic between Great Bear and Great Slave Lakes. Twice I heard from Indians that the wolverine not only could and would attack a man, but had; that certain travelers lost in the Arctic were presumed to have been gobbled up by wolverines. There is, however, not one verified or even convincing report of such an incident. Caught in a trap, a wolverine would resist ferociously, and a female could be expected to defend her den and young, but the notion of a wolverine stalking and overpowering a man is fantasy, the stuff of which travelers' tales are made.

Finally there are stories, again some of them true, of wolverines breaking into trappers' cabins, ripping open food stores, destroying pelts, fouling them with musk, dragging them off into the bush. This behavior would be in keeping with the nature of a wolverine. Coming across a cabin, particularly one from which came the scent of food, he would be inclined to investigate. Being as powerful as he is, the wolverine would be able to break into almost any log cabin. Once inside, a wolverine could be expected to create havoc, to befoul what he did not eat, to try to drag off some of the booty and store it for future use. But again, myths have emerged from the facts. The wolverine, which is sometimes called devil bear and demon, is thought by many Indians to be an evil spirit, not an animal. The demon breaks into a cabin, wrecks it, robs a trapper's sets, not because he is a hunter but because he hates man, is forever looking for a chance to terrorize and humiliate him, drive him out of his territory. The wolverine is of course no more capable of or moved by such diabolical feelings than is the mouse who chews off the corner of a cracker box in the cupboard.

Stories about the ferocious, malicious, unnatural behavior of wolverines have persisted perhaps, for as much as any other reason, because one of the rewards of traveling in far, lonely places is being able to return and raise the hair on the heads of stay-at-homes with tales of the dangers and curiosities one has encountered. A man who has spent a year or two in the Arctic is perhaps entitled to the pleasure of telling a few wolverine stretchers. In addition, it remains hard to separate wolverine fact from fiction because the animal inhabits such inhospitable regions that it has been difficult for naturalists to make accurate observations of his behavior. Less is known about the habits and life style of this animal than any other large predator in North America.

Because he is one of the few naturalists with the opportunity and patience to study wolverines closely over a long period of time, Peter Krott, an Austrian, has written one of the few good descriptions of this animal. Krott spent several years in Finland and Sweden, observing wild wolverines, raising young animals in captivity, releasing them, continuing to follow them when they reverted to the wild. His book *Demon of the North* (the title is a spoof on many of the wild tales told about wolverines) is an excellent and entertaining one.

Among other things, Krott discovered that the wolverine was by nature no more savage or dangerous than any other well-armed mammal and rather than being filled with hatred for man, was, under the proper circumstances, more friendly and affectionate than many wild creatures. During the course of his study, Krott raised half a dozen young wolverines in his home. They were given the free run of the house and were playmates of Krott's infant son. As the animals grew older they were still allowed their freedom and encouraged to wander off on their own, since one of the purposes of the study was to observe the animals under natural conditions. Even after they had matured and began hunting for themselves, the home-raised wolverines would occasionally return freely to the Krotts, not to wreck havoc, but apparently out of affection.

The chances of anyone studying a wolverine, even seeing one in the continental United States, are very slim. The only place they are still reported is in the high mountains of the Northwest and even there they are very scarce. There are certainly less than a hundred animals left, and some estimates place the population at only a dozen pairs. Northward in Canada and Alaska (and around the Arctic Circle, since the wolverine is found in both Asia and Europe) they are more numerous, but are no place common and by all reports growing scarcer everywhere.

A partial explanation for the scarcity of wolverines is a familiar one. The wolverine, like so many other large predators, has come in conflict with man and has lost. The present scarcity, virtual extinction, of the wolverine in the continental United States is largely the work of man, European man. First, as has been noted so many times previously, we have altered the environment, reduced, changed, tamed the wilderness, and the wolverine is very much a wilderness animal. We have trapped and shot the wolverine until only a remnant population is left.

Throughout most of the history of the fur trade, wolverine fur has been bought and sold, but it has seldom been of exceptional value, being rough and coarse. However, though wolverines have never been a great prize for trappers, there has always been some market for their pelts, and trappers have taken them often almost accidentally because they are easy to trap. Like the fisher, the marten, and for that matter most of the mustelids, the wolverine, because of his curiosity, aggressiveness, lack of fear, is notably unwary of traps. He can be taken by most baits in an open set. In recent years wolverine fur has increased in popularity and trapping has become a greater threat to the animals remaining. While it is not particularly attractive in appearance, wolverine fur does have one useful property: the coarse hairs shed moisture, do not collect frost. For this reason arctic residents and travelers have always valued it as a liner for the opening of parka hoods. Whereas in the arctic winter a man's breath would quickly turn another fur into a mass of ice, the moisture will not freeze and collect on wolverine trim. In the past several decades the enormous growth in the popularity of skiing and other winter sports has increased the demand for cold-weather clothing and with it, for wolverine-trimmed parkas.

There is a greater demand now for wolverine pelts than there ever has been. In consequence, trappers who formerly took wolverines more or less by accident, because they were easy to trap, are now more interested in these animals. Currently about two thousand wolverine skins a year are sold, a substantial number considering that even in its northern range the wolverine is not plentiful.

Trapping aside, men have also persistently killed wolverines, as they have other large predators, because they have regarded them as a danger to wild game or domestic stock. In the early years of the settlement of this continent, when men were trying to survive, they farmed in small areas surrounded by wilderness. Wolverines may then have been a minor menace to stock and there would have been some reason for destroying animals found near settlements. However, those days are long gone. The wolverines quickly retreated to deep wilderness areas, and have not been a threat to livestock for a century or more.

Despite this, men have gone out of their way to shoot the remaining animals. Beyond the general dislike for predators there is another reason, well illustrated by the case of the wolverine, but a reason which I think is important to understand in connection with the prospects of all our large predators. For many years the wolverine has been a very rare animal—a great curiosity. This has made him more desirable to hunters; he has been shot simply because he is rare, a curiosity.

Perhaps I can best explain this attitude by describing an incident in which I was involved several years ago in northern Minnesota. I was in a small-town hardware store, talking with some residents of the area about reports that a few timber wolves had drifted across the Canadian border into that state. Only one of the men in the conversation had actually seen one of these wolves. This man was a veteran sport hunter who spent a lot of time in the northern woods. "Last fall," he said, "I was at a deer stand when one of those fellows broke across a clearing in front of me. I'd never seen one before, and to be truthful I didn't really know what it was at first. So I shot him. Then I found out he was one of them wolves we've been talking about. Boy was that exciting!"

This reaction—if you meet some strange, unusual, unknown wild thing, kill it—is very widespread. In addition to reflecting the traditional pleasure man receives from taking trophies, it seems to me to be a sad indication that we are becoming less at ease with the natural world, more timid, ignorant about it. However, good or bad, I think many, perhaps most men who go out with guns into the woods would have done as the Minnesota man did. If they met a wolf or other curious beast, they would have killed or at least tried to kill it. This is the principal reason why I am very pessimistic about the prospects of any of our large predators— pumas, wolves, bears, lynx—surviving except in well-guarded sanctuaries which are in a sense large outdoor zoos. I think this is

148

particularly true of the wolverines, the rarest of all the large predators. The wolverine is a wide-ranging animal and it is not impossible that from time to time one will travel down to our northern forests from Canada. However, I think it most unlikely, because of this kill-the-curious reaction, that wolverines will ever re-establish themselves in their former range.

There is little question that the economic needs of man, real and imagined, as well as his psychological quirks have brought about the elimination of the wolverine. However, there is another puzzle with regard to the status and distribution of this animal that has nothing to do with man, and is worth considering since it involves a biological mystery that touches on the lives and our understanding of many other animals, particularly the predators. The puzzle may be described in this way. The wolverine is one of the best-equipped predators in the world. He is large, swift, strong, aggressive enough to prey on virtually any animal on this continent. At the same time, there is no other predator, except man, who threatens the wolverine. The wolverine is anything but a finicky eater, accepting a wide range of food. Finally, the animal is hardy, able to withstand the rigors of a harsh climate. Nevertheless, the wolverine is not a very successful animal. As biologists use the term, the success of a species is usually measured by the extent of its range, *i.e.,* how widely the animal is distributed, and by the numbers of individual animals found within the range. Despite his many apparent advantages, the wolverine is not and never has been plentiful, according to observations of early naturalists, trappers, Indian lore. He is found irregularly across the northern tier of states and in times past ranged farther south only in the eastern and western mountains. Even in the heartland of his territory—the arctic and subarctic regions—the wolverine is not common. Why should this be? Why should such an able animal be so apparently unsuccessful in terms of numbers and range.

We simply do not know the answer to this paradox, and it is an important one, since it also concerns species other than the wolverine. Why an animal lives where he does and not elsewhere, why he is common or uncommon, are the teasing and significant mysteries of natural history. As of now we have no firm answers to these questions, only speculation.

In the case of the wolverine, several theories have been advanced to explain why he is uncommon even in the Far North. Even for a good hunter life is difficult in the arctic regions. Food is scarce throughout much of the year. Both prey and predator species must travel far, work hard simply to keep alive. The hardships of the north tend to depress populations. Therefore there is not much pressure on the wolverine to expand his range, and in fact there are seldom enough wolverines to serve as pioneers.

It has also been suggested that social factors may account for the scarcity of wolverines. From the small amount of evidence available, the wolverine is not a prolific breeder. Two or three young seem to be an average litter, and it may well be that females do not raise a litter every year. One reason for this may simply be lack of opportunity. The wolverine hunts over an enormous territory and is by nature a solitary animal who does not tolerate others of his kind in his territory. Under these circumstances the accidental loss of an adult wolverine could well mean that his or her nearest surviving neighbor might go unmated for several seasons.

As to why the wolverine is, seems always to have been, found only in an arctic or subarctic environment, there is again no completely satisfactory explanation. When an animal is associated with a particular climate or special environment, the obvious thought is that, for some reason, he must remain where he is, cannot cope with other conditions. Perhaps there is something about the arctic, the cold regions, which is essential for the survival of the wolverine. Perhaps there is, but still there are many unanswered questions. For example, many of the smaller mustelids—the otter, weasels, mink—share much of the wolverine's northern range but at the same time thrive far to the south and are found all the way to subtropical areas. If a mink, in some ways a more specialized animal than the wolverine, can inhabit a continent-wide range, why can't the wolverine?

There is still another paradox of this sort. Generally, animals adapted to northern living seem to adjust to warmer climates more readily than southern animals do to cold climates. The polar bear, the most arctic of the predatory mammals, can be kept in captivity in such subtropical places as the Washington, D.C., zoo. A jaguar, on the other hand, would not be able to survive in the open through a Fairbanks, Alaska, winter. Wolverines are occasionally seen in southern zoos and do not seem to suffer excessively from the heat. However, the wolverine in captivity in temperate regions does seem vulnerable to a variety of diseases, which suggests one explanation of why the animal has a relatively restricted range.

The arctic and subarctic climate functions in some ways as a freezer does in the home, impeding the growth and spread of various microscopic plants and animals, bacteria, viruses, molds, some of which may cause decay, infection, disease. The north is a relatively sterile land. It is possible that for the wolverine there is some arbitrary "disease line" closely associated with temperature zones. South of such a line the animal may be exposed to infectious ailments not present in the north, and against which he has little natural immunity. While this sounds plausible, it still does not explain why many of his near relatives seem to thrive as well in the south as the north.

The problem of why the wolverine is found where he is and not in other places where it seems he might survive equally well is complicated by several special circumstances. First there is our ignorance of the animal's habits, and secondly the pressure man has applied to the animal, the vendetta we have waged against him. However, the same mystery, that of seemingly inexplicable distribution patterns, arises in connection with other animals who are relatively easy to study and have apparently not been greatly affected by the activity of man. There are at least two such examples involving animals found in the central Appalachian Mountains near where I now live.

The porcupine is found throughout New England. In the mountains his range extends southward into Pennsylvania, the higher elevations, since they offer food and cover similar to what the porcupine finds in the northern part of his range. However, in mid-Pennsylvania there is quite a sharp demarcation line, north of which there are porcupines, south of which there are none. In obvious ways—climate, vegetation, unoccupied space—the territory below the line seems as suitable for porcupines as that above, but for some subtle reason it is not.

The northern water shrew—the small insectivorous hunter that we were seeking in Cranesville Swamp on the morning we met the mink—serves as another example of this phenomenon. The water shrew is a moderately common animal in the northern tier of states, inhabiting small ponds, free flowing, white water streams and brooks. For one reason or another he has interested a number of naturalists, including myself. We have found that his range extends a considerable distance southward, with the most southerly point being in the Great Smokies National Park in the North Carolina–Tennessee mountains. Again the high mountains duplicate the kind of environment one finds in the more northern states. However, the peculiarity about the distribution of the water shrew is that the farther south he goes, the narrower his range becomes. From southern Pennsylvania southward the water shrew has only been found in a very narrow band, a series of ridges which roughly follow what is called the Allegheny Front, the main elevation of the Appalachians.

For example, after more time than seems reasonable to devote to such a small creature, several friends and myself collected a water shrew along a stream in Huntington County, Pennsylvania, and at least one other has been reported from that area. However, we have devoted even more time to trying to find a water shrew in Adams County, where I now live and which lies about seventy-five miles to the east of Huntington. The streams in Adams County seem to run as fast, have the same temperature, provide the same food resources as those of Huntington County, but so far as we know there are no shrews. It is, of course, possible that we have simply been unable to find them. However, I think this unlikely. The water shrew and his range has intrigued a small but serious group of naturalists. New reports on the presence of these shrews are normally published, and those of us who share this interest also keep in touch informally. The experience of all has been similar. In the southern mountains, for some reason, you find water shrews along the Allegheny Front but you do not find them fifty miles away in country that appears to be identical.

This question of range is one of many unsolved natural-history puzzles. We cannot adequately explain why porcupines, water shrews, wolverines live where they do and not elsewhere, either because we lack sufficient information about the nature and behavior of these animals or perhaps because we lack the wit and imagination to interpret the information we do have. It is well for everybody, those with both a casual and professional interest in natural history to recognize that many such mysteries remain. In the first place, the admission that there is much we do not know, do not understand, goads us into seeking solutions, expanding our knowledge.

Secondly, recognizing our ignorance promotes a very useful sort of humility, prevents us from becoming overly dogmatic in defending existing theories and explanations. As an example: Considerable thought and study have been given to the relationship between prey and predators. In previous chapters, the conventional, accepted theories regarding this phenomenon have been described. Predators help to control the number and distribution of their prey by feeding upon them. The prey performs the same useful, necessary service for the predators by refusing to be fed upon—refusing to be prey. The result is a constructive relationship which enables a variety of species, an optimum number of vigorous individuals, to survive. So far as it goes, these observations, this explanation seem accurate. However, in considering such theories we must avoid the smug notion that this is all there is to know about the predator-prey relationship, all we need to know. The puzzle of the wolverine's range suggests that there are other subtle factors which influence the distribution, population, relationships between species.

Using the example of the wolverine, it would seem that while the factors restricting his numbers and range may be complex, they are necessary, an integral part of the system whereby life supports life. If the wolverine were as common and widely distributed as the skunk, he might, being such a formidable hunter, seriously upset the constantly teetering balance of nature, much as the mongoose did when he was artificially introduced to Jamaica. Every indication is that the wolverine is controlled as a result of an efficient, constructive, if mysterious (to us), cause and effect sequence. It is inconceivable that his restriction is accidental, unconnected with the affairs of other living things.

The questions of why a water shrew lives on one stream and not on another fifty miles to the east, why wolverines are to be found north of Great Slave Lake but not south of Lake Michigan, may seem academic, relatively trivial. However, the fact that we do not really know the answers to these questions indicates that there is a great deal we do not know about the relationships between species and the relationship of all living things to their environment. For intensely practical reasons, we men, with our enormous capacity for altering environment and biological relationships, need to know everything we can about the subject. We cannot afford to ignore or dismiss even trivial-appearing mysteries of this sort. It is essential that we admit our ignorance in environmental matters, seek to remedy it not just for the sake of the handful of surviving wolverines, but for the sake of the billions of men who hope to survive.

The Otters

Among men, the river otter has a better reputation than have any of the other mustelids, better in fact than almost any other predator. Several factors account for the high esteem in which the otter is usually held. Being an aquatic predator, most of his hunting and killing takes place in or under the water, and the bulk of his diet is made up of fish, amphibians, crustaceans, and other cold-blooded creatures. Hunters and farmers who so heartily, often irrationally, dislike the other mustelids, do not regard the otter as a competitor. Many, in fact, are unaware that he is even a member of the terrible weasel clan. Also, because of where and what he kills, the otter, unlike many other predators, does not offend the delicate sensibilities of man, the master killer. Somehow a weasel killing a rabbit strikes many people as a wicked act, while an otter crunching up a sucker does not. As a rule, the fate of cold-blooded animals seldom concerns us.

In addition to these somewhat negative virtues—"he is not, or at least is not like a bloodthirsty weasel"—there are positive reasons for the otter being liked. Perhaps the chief one is that otters are popularly known as very playful animals, and in the human

156

system of values, playfulness is generally thought to be a good characteristic.

The notion that the otter is playful is not false, as are so many of the labels we pin on animals. However, it is a little misleading, since it suggests that playfulness is a characteristic peculiar to the otter, which it is not. Nearly every mammal and many other animals play, that is engage in some sort of activity that might be called frivolous inasmuch as it is not immediately necessary for survival.

Playfulness in otters takes many forms. Young otters, like so many young mammals, particularly predators, are constantly teasing one another, wrestling, chasing after each other in what appear to be tag games. Otters, despite their webbed feet, are very "handy" animals, and both adult and young animals will amuse themselves for long periods of time fondling, tossing, feeling all manner of objects—stones, sticks, bits of weed. A friend of mine fishing in an Ontario lake reported spending most of his afternoon watching a full-grown otter who spent most of his afternoon floating on his back in the water, playing with a duck feather.

Otters amuse themselves in many ways, but they have earned their reputation as playboys of the animal world because of one particular habit. The best-known game of otters is sliding down banks, snow banks, mud banks, grass banks, on their stomachs. That this activity should so often be cited as proof that otters are exceptionally playful animals is not surprising. Many animals' games don't look like games to us because they involve equipment, skills, attitudes, which we do not have. However, anybody who has gone down a sliding board, ski run, worn holes in his pants sliding down a ravine, can appreciate and identify with the otters' game.

So popular is this activity with otters that where you find inclines and otters you are likely to find otter slides. One summer on a small lake in Michigan I had a chance to watch the construction of an otter playground, and occasionally the otters at play. In and around this lake were deposits of marl, a slippery clay that contains a large amount of lime. Because of the lime, marl is often used as a fertilizer. Marl had once been dug commercially along the shore of this lake, but operations had ceased years before. What remained were a number of large pits, whose sides rose ten or fifteen feet above the level of the water. That particular summer in some lakeside den an otter had borne at least three young. (Three young were all that were in the family when I met them.) Inevitably, given the nature of otters, the family discovered the inviting marl cliffs.

There was one isolated marl bank where water running off from the overgrown fields above had commenced to erode a small furrow. As I read the signs, the otters, either by design or accident, came across this spot during their wanderings. For a time they occupied themselves by climbing the bank, then running, tumbling down it, following the tiny erosion crevice. Within several weeks after they discovered the spot, they had worn out a proper slide, a narrow otter-width groove. By the end of the summer this was nearly a foot deep, very much like the cross section of a tunnel. On each side of the slide there were numerous small paths, worn in the soft marl, which the otters used for ascending the bank.

Twice during the summer, both times early in the morning, I found the otters at play, and from a canoe anchored offshore was able to watch them. The mother, who weighed about fifteen

pounds, used the slide, but neither as frequently nor as enthusi-astically as her offspring. Every now and then she would scramble up the side of the bank, and on the slippery marl it was hard going at times for the larger animal, and slide down into the water. After one of her trips she spent a good bit of time groom-ing herself, combing the sticky clay from her coat. When the sun hit the cove, she was content for long periods to sunbathe, doze, either in the water or on the shore. The three young, who were about the size of elongated muskrats, appeared to have nothing on their mind but getting as many turns on the slide as possible.

Many animals, notably the Mustelidae, are accused of going berserk when it comes to killing, of being gripped with a kind of bloodlust, a frenzy which seems to addle their normal wits and instincts. Occasionally this may happen, but it is probably a very rare occurrence, much rarer than stories supposedly describing it. However, based on my observations of this otter family, I tend to believe that animals can be overwhelmed by play lust. It seems to me that this is a fair way to describe the actions, the mood, of the three young otters. They were frantic to get up to the top, then come down their slide. As they scrambled up they squeaked, yipped, growled in excitement. At the top they would hurl them-selves into the slide, give a few starting pushes with their paws, streak down it, hit the water, hardly pause before rushing out and up to the top again. The longer they slid, the more slippery the run became, the water from their fur giving the soft marl a grease-like coating. The faster they went, the more frenzied they became. Often one pup in his excitement would attempt to climb back to the top using the slide itself and he inevitably would meet head-on one of the others coming down. Such collisions resulted in some ferocious sounding, but harmless quarrels. Usually the sliding pup, with momentum in his favor, was able to knock aside the climbing one, but occasionally, as they wrestled and swore at each other, both would come down to the water together. Like a human mother at a playground, the female would appear after a time to become restless, would swim out into the lake, come back, chirp at the pups as if to tell them it was time to go. However, she didn't have much luck until the pups became thoroughly exhausted.

While what the family of otters did on the marl bank looked like play, and has commonly been called play for as long as men have been watching otters, most serious students of animal behavior would have, up until a few years ago, warned that this activity should not be called play. The reasoning was based on a fundamental assumption regarding the difference between men and other animals. In the past decades this assumption has been challenged but still has a great influence, not only on how we view the play of otters but animal behavior in general.

Briefly, this assumption is that when it comes to behavior man is different from all other creatures. We are unique because of our intellect, rationality, powers of abstraction. Man is a learning animal—what he learns, his individual experience, largely determines how he will behave. Other animals, so the assumption went, act as they do because of their instincts—inherited reactions, behavior patterns. An animal has no more control over his instincts —and thus his behavior—than he does over the length of his tail. Both his instincts and his tail are evolved characteristics. They evolved because for one reason or another they contributed to the survival of the species, made the individual animal better able to deal with his environment, meet the competition of other creatures. Therefore the meaning and motives behind any particular type of animal behavior can only be explained in terms of the survival value of that behavior.

With regard to the otter family on a mud slide, these assumptions lead to the following conclusion. Men can properly be said to play when they slide down a hill bceause they can choose (because of their unique mental, emotional equipment, ability to learn) to engage in what is essentially a frivolous activity. An otter slides down a bank because he has inherited the instinct to do so. In this activity otters develop and practice skills which they need as hunters—thus the habit has survival value. To say that the otter plays, as we say a man plays, is inaccurate because we are assigning human motives and meaning to the action.

In the last several decades the findings of many ethnologists (students of inherited behavior), anthropologists, psychologists, have raised doubts about this neat, if rather rigid, theory. In the first place, it now seems that it is inaccurate, arrogant, to speak, as we so long have, of man as being *the* rational animal. We are very probably the most rational animal, our behavior seems to be more influenced by what we learn than that of any other species. However, all animals are to a degree rational in the sense that they do learn from their individual experiences and are influenced by them. Also it seems to many scientists that more of our own habits, behavior patterns, may be "instinctive" than was assumed. Thus jealousy, possessiveness, many patterns of social aggression and cooperation, may be inherited rather than learned.

Generally speaking, it seems that the dividing line between men and other animals is not so sharp or clear-cut as it was formerly believed to be. For example, studies of chimpanzees, dogs, and other animals indicate that they are emotional creatures, as much or perhaps more so than man. They seem to be moved by anger, jealousy, loyalty, humor, friendship, fear, and combinations of these emotions. Similarly, it has been an article of faith that only man is intellectual, imaginative, abstractive, perhaps frivolous enough to be concerned with beauty. However, now there is some evidence and much speculation that other animals may also have aesthetic needs, seek out certain sounds, scenes, shapes, situations, principally because they give what can only be called sensual pleasure.

There is also a growing reluctance to try to explain all types of animal behavior in terms of survival value. In the very long run perhaps every action of every animal, including man, may reflect the fundamental drive of all creatures to live as long as they can and as well as they can. However, trying to demonstrate that each action of an individual animal is made in response to the survival instinct seems to be a pointlessly complicated exercise. Perhaps sliding does have, or once had, some survival value for otters (as it may or may not have had for men), but it tortures both logic and fact to insist that an otter slides to survive. There is as much or more reason to assume that the otter slides for about the same motives as a boy does—because both have a need (instinctive or learned) for stimulation, sensation, excitement, in short, fun, and sliding satisfies this need.

The willingness of scientists in various fields to consider the possibility that a boy and an otter sliding down a bank may have something in common is one reason why the field of animal behavior is becoming one of the most important and exciting modern studies. Until recently, what might be called the inner life of animals was assumed to be either nonexistent or, if it existed, to be a bleak, blank, mechanistic thing not worth exploring. Now many feel otherwise. There seems too much to discover in this area and it is likely that many of these discoveries will be important and practical, not only because they increase our knowledge of what other animals are, but because they may give us new insights into what we men are, enable us to better understand the meaning of our own behavior, our motives. For men, the most rational animals, self-knowledge has immense survival value.

Assuming that it is proper to speak of the otter as being what he appears to be, a playful animal, another explanation of why this is so may be that the otter is relatively social, more social than any of the other mustelids except perhaps the badger. This sociability may very well contribute to the otter's playfulness. Animals, like men, are more inclined to play in groups than alone.

The social unit for otters is the family. A mother otter and her young stay together for a long time and play together. Occasionally it seems two female otters with pups will join forces, travel together, raise their families jointly. Very rarely does the father remain with the family group. Young otters are whelped in midspring. Normally the den is a burrow at the edge of the water, often an enlarged muskrat tunnel. Sometimes a hollow tree will be used, and in marshy lands where no other cover is available, the female will pull together reeds and other vegetation to make a sort of wigwam for her pups. The pups stay in or about the home den until they are a month or so old. Young otters when they set out into the big watery world have a lot to learn. Among other things they are not very strong swimmers. A mother otter sometimes carries very young pups on her back, often floats in the water while her young cling to her, use her somewhat like children will use a diving raft, as a place to rest, catch their breath. The family group stays together throughout the summer, often until the next spring, when the mother bears another litter. Occa-

sionally yearling otters who have not mated will hunt and travel together for several years. Because of this domestic pattern, female otters are seldom alone during their lifetime. They are with their litter mates when they are young, and after maturity usually are with their own pups. Males, however, eventually drift off to lead essentially solitary lives. However, even mature males seem a bit more social than is usual among the mustelids. They will occasionally meet up with females and young, travel with them for a time, join them at a mud slide, then move on.

Males also keep in touch (or, more accurately, in smell) with other otters in the vicinity by leaving messages for them. The otter, like another aquatic mammal, the beaver, will make a small mound of mud and grass, sprinkle it with a few drops of musk. These little mounds serve as a means of communication between otters, passing along information as to who has gone where. They also very probably are a means of advertising for mates or warning off competitors from a territory.

Before leaving the subject of the otter's sociability, it is worth noting that these animals make good pets, and if taken young, adjust more easily to man than almost any other wild predator. The observation of many who have kept these animals is that they can be treated and respond much like a dog. Rather than living a life of a surly prisoner, as many wild animals in captivity do, otters, again because they are gregarious by nature, seem to develop considerable affection for humans. This of course assumes that the man treats them not like a prisoner but with affection. (It should be noted that those who have had the best experiences with otters have been able to let their pets wander with a considerable amount of freedom. Otters are great travelers. The chances of an otter regarding with affection a man who keeps him in a small cage are slight.) There have been many instances of otters being successfully kept as pets, but perhaps the classic man-otter story was told by Gavin Maxwell in his book *Ring of Bright Water*. Anyone with an interest in wildlife should read Maxwell's book, not only for the information it provides about otters, but also because there are few better accounts of how a man and animal can come to understand each other, and the rewards of such understanding, at least for the man.

In addition to making good pets, otters have the distinction of being one of the few predators outside the dog family with whom man has entered into what might be called a working partnership. Several otter keepers, making use of the otter's intelligence, obedience, and superior skill in the water, have trained these animals to retrieve waterfowl brought down by a gun. Those who have done so report that the otter is much more efficient at this work than a dog. This is not surprising since even the best of retrieving dogs are still essentially dry-land animals. Also, once an otter learns what is expected of him, he appears to enjoy the exercise thoroughly. One problem of hunting with an otter seems to be restraining him from retrieving everything in sight, not only ducks but sticks, stones, hunting jackets, and lunches.

Beyond what might be called his character, certainly the most distinctive thing about the otter is his marvelous skill in the water. No other inland mammal can match the otter's aquatic ability. The beaver and the muskrat are good swimmers, but compared to an otter they are as trucks are to racing cars. The otter is built, equipped, to go fast and far, in or under the water (otters can swim a quarter of a mile without coming up for air). The otter's cousin, the mink, is also an aquatic predator, but whereas the mink will sometimes by stealth catch a few fish in the shallows, only the otter among all the mammals is able simply to "swim-down" a fish in open water.

The otter is superbly equipped as an aquatic hunter because of a number of special physical adaptations. In the first place, like the other slim-bodied mustelids, he is long, lithe, streamlined. This, so far as speed and maneuverability go, gives him considerable advantage over such chunky aquatic rodents as the beaver and muskrat. However, unlike any other mustelid, the otter has fully webbed feet on both his hind and forepaws. The otter's tail, which is long, tapered, strong, serves as an admirable rudder. Underneath his skin the otter's body is encased in a layer of fat—just as are the seals, whales, and other marine mammals. This blubber serves as insulation and enables the otter to operate throughout the year as far north as the Arctic. The otter's pelt also provides special and effective insulation. The undercoat is thick, fine, soft. The outer coat is made up of relatively rough guard hairs. When the otter submerges, air clings to these guard hairs and the animal is in a sense encased in a film of insulating bubbles. For this reason an otter swimming underwater has the look of a silvery projectile, with a glittering wake trailing behind. The silvery appearance comes from the bubbles on his guard hair, and the wake from the escaping air.

So far as predation is concerned, the otter's chief equipment are his broad, strong jaws. The teeth are somewhat broader than those of the other mustelids, and with them the otter is able to, and often does, grind up turtles, clams, and other shell-encased creatures. Though his feet are webbed, the otter is deft with his paws, and as mentioned previously, seems to enjoy fondling small objects such as pebbles, sticks, shells, feathers. Otters also spend a lot of time grooming their coats, as do most aquatic mammals, combing, drying their fur with their paws. Also, almost monkey-like, members of an otter family will often groom each other.

The otter is able to prey on almost any creature found in inland waters. However, the bulk of an otter's diet is made up of fish and shellfish. He is quite capable of taking waterfowl, muskrat, beaver, even his near relative the mink, but does not appear to do so regularly. Often otters are found living in active beaver ponds or muskrat colonies, sharing the water in relative peace with the rodents. Popularly, such situations have been cited as evidence that the otter is an agreeable, "good," animal. If you are thinking in the beavers' terms rather than fishes' (as we tend to do), there may be certain truth in this observation, inasmuch as the otter seems to be somewhat less aggressive than the weasel, mink, and other mustelids. However, it seems unlikely that the otter has any moral scruples against taking a beaver, muskrat, or duck. That he only occasionally preys on these creatures probably serves again to verify the fact that hunting animals tend to hunt the prey that is easiest, least risky—in the case of the otter, fish. It could well be that the otter simply likes fish better than beaver, as a man may prefer lobster to steak. Otters are also, to a greater extent than many of the mustelids, vegetarians, frequently digging out, feeding on, the roots of lillies and other aquatic plants.

Though specially adapted to live and hunt in the water, the otter, unlike many of the marine predators, is by no means helpless out of the water. With his webbed feet and short legs, the otter is not particularly graceful on land but he is an effective and enduring traveler, loping along with the typical weasel gait, mile after mile. In the course of his roamings, the otter undoubtedly sometimes preys on land creatures—rabbits, mice, birds, insects—but generally speaking when an otter is hungry, when the time comes to hunt seriously, he returns to the water.

Both by land and water, the otter is known as one of the great travelers among North American mammals. A family of otters, mother and young, will regularly patrol five miles or so of lakeshore or riverbank in the course of a night, and solitary males may travel ten or fifteen miles. Sometimes, particularly in winter, otters will make trips of fifty or sixty miles, going overland from one drainage system to the other, in the process climbing steep ridges, even mountains, pushing through thickets and snowdrifts.

The otter is surprisingly efficient in the deep snow. With his short legs he, in a sense, swims, paddles through the snow, rather than walking over it.

In my area of the central Appalachians there are few otters left. The remaining ones are a great prize for fur trappers, but I know only one trapper who regularly takes a few otter pelts each year. Like many other trappers, he makes a trip to Virginia each winter, one of the few eastern areas where there is much chance of finding otters. However, unlike most other trappers, this man usually gets what he goes after, at least one otter skin. Knowing that I am no competition, he once explained to me the secret of his success. He said that after following otters for years he had discovered what he called an "otter road," a circuitous trail leading from the Rapidan to Rappahannock River, a distance of some thirty miles. Every winter, so this trapper claims, there is considerable travel back and forth on this same trail. "The rest of them," he says somewhat contemptuously of other trappers, "mess around down in the swamps. I go up on the ridge on that old road, stay just as dry as you please and get my otter."

The trapper had no intention of showing me the road or giving me any precise directions as to where to find it. Trappers, particularly when it comes to something as rare, difficult, and valuable as an otter, tend to be secretive, devious. It is possible that the whole story of an otter road across the mountain ridge is fiction, but it could well be a fact. Given the otter's known inclination to travel, his sociability, habit of leaving scent markers, such roads, used by generation after generation of the animals, may exist.

What makes an otter roam as he does is a mystery. The otter, peculiarly adapted to the water, which offers excellent shelter and almost inexhaustible food supplies, would seem to be an unlikely traveler. He does not appear to have the practical need to roam. Quite probably the reasons will remain a mystery until we learn more than we now know about the inner life of animals. Perhaps, as he has a need to play, the otter, like a man, has a need to travel because he is restless, curious, needs stimulation, a change of scenery, enjoys the experience.

Whatever the reason or motive, the fact that the otter is a great traveler unquestionably accounts in part for his wide distribution. Until relatively recent times otters were found virtually everywhere in what is now the United States, from the Mexican border to the Alaskan Arctic. They were always closely associated with water. Even in such unpromising areas as the southwest there were some otters hunting along the bigger rivers, retreating in dry times to deep pools, often managing to survive in almost desert areas.

Though they were found practically everywhere, otters, like many other medium-to-large predators who require a sizable territory, were apparently never numerous in any one locality. Their wanderings, the unavailability of mates, the fact that young otters mature rather slowly, all probably contribute to a low reproductive rate. Because of the naturally low density of the otter population the species is especially vulnerable to any crisis which disrupts the environment, creates hazardous conditions for individual animals. For example, if a particular river valley is inhabited by ten otters, the loss or migration of four of the animals, especially if they happen to be mature individuals capable of breeding, might all but eliminate otters from that locality. In the same valley there might well be a hundred muskrats. The loss of forty of these animals would do little more than momentarily reduce the colony, the remaining breeding stock being sufficient to restore the population to its former level in a season or so.

The coming of European man did, of course, create such a disruptive crisis for the otter. First, as has been repeatedly noted, we altered the environment. The otter was particularly vulnerable in this regard, for despite the fact that the animal is widely distributed he is an environmental specialist, dependent upon water, and water is a natural resource which man has meddled with excessively.

By damming, draining, impounding for human use, we have reduced the amount of free water available, and in doing so, reduced by millions of acres the suitable otter habitat on the continent. Perhaps even more seriously, we have poisoned much of the remaining free water with the various waste products of civilization. No one has measured accurately how water pollution affects living creatures. However, in a general way we know the effects to be adverse. Even though the otter himself may be able to tolerate pollution, the aquatic creatures he thrives on cannot.

As it did for so many of the mustelids, the coming of European man, specifically the fur hunter with his traps, presented the otter with a new and formidable natural enemy, a predator that could prey on him more effectively and persistently than any had before. The pressure was particularly heavy on the otter, since his fur is especially valuable, otter skins sometimes having sold for as much as a hundred dollars apiece.

The results of these environmental changes and persistent human predation on this widely, but thinly, distributed species was inevitable. Now, except in certain areas of the southwest, notably Louisiana, and in Alaska, the otter is a very rare animal, and there are large areas where the otter appears to be extinct.

Despite the fact that his existence is threatened, his long term hopes for survival may be better than that of some of the other large predators. Because he is a valuable furbearer, experiments are now being made, as they have been with the mink and other of the mustelids, aimed at raising the otter in captivity. The establishment of commercial otter ranches, along with effectively enforced bans on trapping, could relieve much of the direct, predatory pressure on the remaining population of wild otters. Also, unlike many of the large predators, the otter seems to adjust to the presence of man rather easily. Occasionally otters turn up in surprising places, near cities, around heavily populated resorts. By the same token, man seems to adjust rather easily to the presence of otters. Because this animal is regarded as an agreeable, harmless, noncompetitive one, men are more likely to tolerate an otter, even go out of their way to protect it, as they will not other predators. If trapping can be controlled, small otter populations might survive, even be re-established, quite close to large human populations.

Ultimately the question of whether or not the otter can survive rests on a larger matter which involves the survival of many other species. Can we (and the responsibility is obviously man's) maintain an inhabitable environment? No matter how kindly we may feel toward otters, no matter what laws may be passed to protect him, the otter will continue to dwindle in numbers, eventually disappear, if we continue to poison water at the rate we now are. The hazards of water pollution are so serious to all life that it is a little ridiculous to argue that we must cease poisoning our rivers, lakes, streams so as to save the otter. It is ridiculous in much the same way it would be to campaign for the abolition of nuclear weapons because they are a threat to the survival of the remaining fifty whooping cranes.

The story of the sea otter is a short but thought-provoking one. It illustrates not so much the nature of this animal as it does the predatory nature of man, underlines the point that only in man are predatory habits, instincts, skills, sufficiently developed to create a fundamental threat to other species. Only man can or will hunt another species to extinction, as we did in the case of one marine musteline, the sea mink, and as we came very close to doing in the case of the sea otter.

The sea otter is the largest of the American mustelids, weighing as much as eighty pounds. In appearance he resembles an oversized river otter. In habit he is more seal-like, being a marine creature who lives in western coastal waters from the Aleutians to California. Like the seal, the otter will occasionally come on land to a rocky island or promontory, but otherwise his life is spent in the ocean. Like his continental relative, but to an even greater degree, the sea otter is a fish and crustacean eater. He also seems to be a good-natured, playful, restless animal. However, all characteristics, habits, adaptations of the sea otter are, so far as his survival and present status are concerned, subordinate to the fact that his fur is regarded by man as the most beautiful, desirable, in the world. The extraordinarily thick, soft, luxurious coat was evolved to enable the sea otter to survive in the frigid arctic water he inhabits. However, the fact that he possesses a fur that strikes man as extremely desirable brought the otter to the very brink of extinction. He now survives because of this coat, as an absolute ward of man.

Sea otters were known for centuries to American Indians and Asiatic hunters who lived on the shores of the northern Pacific.

174

The skins were admired and sought after, but without, it appears, much adverse effect on the otter population. The reason seems to be that the otters inhabited waters too distant and difficult for the primitive hunters to penetrate in any great numbers.

All of this changed in 1737 when Russian explorers first located sea otter herds in the Aleutian area. For the next one hundred and fifty years, Europeans regularly invaded the northern waters, principally to take the valuable pelts. For example, in the same year, 1786, that he discovered the islands that now bear his name, the Russian explorer Geasim Pribilof brought back five thousand otter skins from the islands. Some two thousand pelts were taken the following season, and since then no sea otters have ever been found on the Pribilof Islands. Two decades later, Russian fur traders slaughtered fifteen thousand otters in one season along the Alaskan coast.

At first, taking the otters who were unalarmed by man, was a very simple matter. Sailors in small boats landed on the rocks used by large otter colonies and killed the animals with clubs by the hundreds and thousands. Later the otters belately grew wary of man, longboat crews pursued the fleeing otters through the water until they were exhausted and could be clubbed or shot. The hunters also discovered and took advantage of the fact that the sea otter, like the river otter, is an affectionate, family animal. Encountering a family the hunters would seek to capture one of the slower, less agile pups. The adult female and the other young in the litter would then try to rejoin the captive and thus make easy prey for the gunners and clubbers.

By the mid-nineteenth century the sea otter population had been drastically reduced in the northern Pacific because of the activities of the Russian traders. The fact that the otter was becoming increasingly scarce contributed to the willingness of the Russians to sell Alaska to the United States in 1867. The record of the American hunters, who began pursuing the herds farther and farther south, was no better than that of the Russians who preceded them. During the decade of the 1880s the Alaska Company (an American firm) took nearly fifty thousand otter skins. This however marked the end of the otter boom, for the excellent reason that the otters were very near their end as a species. In 1900 only one hundred twenty-seven were taken and in 1910, though a fleet of sixteen ships sought them, only thirty skins were secured during the season. That year a single sea otter pelt was sold for two thousand dollars.

In 1911, after the otters had been virtually destroyed, the principal northern Pacific trading nations signed an international agreement protecting the animals. Fur traders made little objection to the treaty, since there were no more otters to be found, legal or illegal. There were long periods during the next quarter of a century when no otters were reported and many observers believed they were extinct in American waters. However in the mid-1930s a small colony was discovered off the California coast and a few small bands were located in the Aleutian Islands. By 1940 it was estimated that the total otter population was somewhat under one thousand individuals. Because protective laws were rigidly enforced, the herd has continued to grow until there may now be as many as thirty thousand otters in American waters. In 1969 the first otter hunt and sale of pelts in fifty-eight years took place. Under close supervision of the Alaska Fish and Game Department, five hundred otter pelts were taken and offered for sale, with the prime pelt of the lot being purchased by a New York furrier for eleven hundred dollars. Future hunts and sales are anticipated, game managers believing that a small number of animals can be regularly harvested without endangering the species' future survival.

The saga of the sea otter, his discovery, decimation, and eventual restoration by "civilized" man is a short one. So is the moral of the story. The sea otter is one of any number of other species that are now absolute hostages of man. If we continue to protect him, the sea otter seems to have a good chance of surviving. If we abandon or relax our protection there seems little doubt that human predation will shortly cause the extinction of the animal. Our power to dominate the environment of this world is enormous. As our power grows, so must our willingness to restrain that power. Restraint is necessary for the sake of the otter and our many other hostages, but also for the sake of ourselves, since we also have the power of self-destruction. We are in a sense our own hostages.

The Black-footed Ferret

One winter I spent several nights on the edge of the South Dakota Badlands, sitting from dusk to dawn in a jeep with a federal biologist named Don Fortenbury watching for black-footed ferrets. One night Don said, in his Kentucky drawl, "A fellow from a zoo wrote me the other day. He said he understood I knew all about black-footed ferrets and he'd appreciate a little information. I wrote back and said if I was supposed to know all about them, I sure would like to meet the fellow who didn't know anything about them."

Most of what I know about the black-footed ferret I learned from Don during those night watches, when we waited on the lee side of a butte but never did see a ferret. On the face of it, this would not seem to establish one as much of an authority on these animals. All that can be said in self-defense is that my credentials are about as good as anyone else's except Don Fortenbury's. Don, despite his disclaimer, knows more about this ferret than any other man knows or is likely to know for some time.

As to sitting up all night not to see a ferret, all I can say is that I am no worse off in this respect than anyone else. Only a handful of naturalists plus a few residents of the Great Plains region have ever seen a living ferret. Furthermore, toward dawn of the second winter night of ferret watching I almost saw one, missed doing so by a mile, and I have always thought of this near miss as something of a triumph.

As you may have guessed, the black-footed ferret is an uncommonly scarce and mysterious animal. This weasel-like mustelid of the Great Plains is generally regarded as the rarest mammal in North America, one of the rarest in the world. The official guess of the United States Fish and Wildlife Service, which is, in a sense, the ferret's guardian, is that there may be about fifty of the animals surviving, but this is nothing more than a rough estimate. Don Fortenbury, whose business it is to see as many ferrets as he can, had, after looking for a year, seen only a dozen of the animals. Whatever the true number, it is very small, and this has apparently been the case for a long time—the ferret, so far as our records go, has always been very rare.

The ferret was the last of the largish North American mammals to be discovered by naturalists. It was first reported and described by John James Audubon in 1849, when the artist was crossing the Great Plains. Promptly after being found, the ferret was lost, at least it was not reported again for almost half a century and there was considerable speculation among biologists as to what, if anything, Audubon, whose reputation for accuracy was not of the highest, had actually seen. However, in the late 1890s several other ferret sightings were made, and the animal has continued to be seen now and then throughout this century. He appeared often enough to keep naturalists looking for him, and infrequently enough to encourage speculation that each report might have been the last, that the ferret had finally become extinct.

Obviously, little has been learned about such an elusive creature. It is difficult to be definite even about the animal's appearance, since there are too few study skins (most museum skins were obtained when animals were picked up that had been killed along highways) to permit any final judgment as to variations in size and markings. In general, however, the ferret resembles a long-necked, oversized mink. The coat is a dusty, yellowish brown. The tip of the tail and paws are black. There is a prominent black mask across the upper muzzle and eyes. Based on specimens that have been studied, the animal resembles the European or domestic ferret more closely than he does any of the other North American mustelids.

The European ferret was orginally a native of the Middle East and North Africa. There, several thousand years ago, it was domesticated and since then has been used all over the world as a ratter and rabbit hunter. Thirty years ago, domestic ferrets were commonly used in this country to flush small game—they popped down a hole to chase out whatever is inside. Based on my own experience with the animals, they are very efficient hunters—and agreeable house pets.

The domestic ferret is much the same color, including a black mask, as the native animal, and though smaller, of the same long, lithe shape. The similarity is close enough to have caused some confusion, and many reports of the rare North American predator turned out, on investigation, to involve escaped domestic ferrets.

As far as its habits are concerned, almost nothing was known about the black-footed ferret until the time Don Fortenbury began to study the animal. One of the few facts generally agreed upon was that the ferret was nearly always found in and around prairie-

dog colonies. The assumption, based on a very few records and the guess that he would tend to behave somewhat like other mustelids, was that he preyed upon these rodents, used their tunnels for dens.

The central mystery of the ferret is his scarcity. The ferret has no obvious handicaps as a predator. He seems to be as well equipped as any of the other mustelids. He is large, apparently strong and quick enough to prey, it would seem, on relatively large rodents, as well as upon such small creatures as mice, ground-nesting birds, insects. At the same time, there is no apparent reason why the ferret should be any more vulnerable to being preyed upon by larger predators than any of the other mustelids. One might expect the ferret occasionally (about as often as the mink) to be preyed upon by his larger relative, the badger, which occupies the same range, but it is unimaginable that predation should be the cause of his rarity.

Finally, the present scarcity of the ferret cannot be accounted for, as that of so many other creatures can, by activities of European man. By all accounts the ferret was very rare when white man first came to the Great Plains. Since then, the ferret has not been trapped. It was so uncommon that most trappers did not know it existed and its pelt is the least desirable of all the mustelids, being coarse, thin, unattractively marked. Furthermore, the ferret, unlike many of his relatives, has not been an object of irrational dislike and prejudice, has not (or at least not often) been killed as a wicked varmint. Again, he has always been so rare that generally speaking he has no reputation at all, good or bad. However, among the few ranchers, farmers, hunters who do know about the animal, he is not known as a threat to domestic stock or game animals. Since it is assumed the ferret feeds largely on prairie dogs, which are often regarded as pests, those who have any opinions at all about the ferret seem to feel that, on the whole, he is a desirable animal.

It is true that in the Great Plains, as everywhere else, the original environment has been altered and this might be thought to have affected the status of the ferret to a degree. However, alterations here have been less drastic than in wooded, watered areas. One would not expect the ferret, who appears to be a relatively unspecialized animal, to be as much affected by environmental alterations as the wolverine, martin, otter, or even the badger and the other, more specialized mustelids of the plains and prairies.

Why the black-footed ferret is so scarce is one of the many wildlife questions for which we have no answer. It is generally believed that at some time in the past the animal was more numerous, more widespread than he has been during the past century or so. No species we know of has evolved and then simply hung on indefinitely, represented by a few dozen or few hundred individuals. An animal so unsuited for survival would not have appeared in the first place. If, as logic indicates, the ferret was once considerably more common than it is now, then about all that can be said is that something happened to the environment, to his relationship with other animals, to the ferret himself, which made him unable to maintain his range and numbers. What this happening was, the cause of the ferret's failure, is one of the questions for which Don Fortenbury is seeking an answer.

Any animal as rare as the black-footed ferret exists in a perpetual state of evolutionary crisis. For such creatures the line between survival and extinction is razor-thin. Because there are so few of them, they cannot absorb, adjust to environmental, ecological change and disruption as more numerous animals can. They have no population reserves, fringe animals to cushion the effects of such shocks. Several years ago such a crisis (which many thought would be the final, fatal one) seemed to be developing for the ferret. While man apparently did not initially force the ferret into his present precarious position, it appeared in the spring of 1965 that men were about to deliver the evolutionary *coup de grâce* to this rare predator. Curiously, the crisis for the ferret was begun and then, at the last moment, averted because of the activities of the United States Fish and Wildlife Service. While this federal agency is generally associated with conservation activities and has a reputation for being the protector of American wildlife, there is at least one division of the Service whose function is quite different. This is the rather misleadingly named Division of Wildlife Services. The old name of this office, the Bureau of Predator Control, was more, though still not entirely, descriptive. Whatever it is called, the organization operates as a federal exterminating service. Each year its agents kill, mostly by poison, a hundred thousand or so native mammals who someone, for one reason or another, believes to be threats to man. Though most responsible conservationists feel these operations are unnecessary, ineffective, based on obsolete biological theories, the work of the federal poisoning agency continues because various powerful groups, chiefly agricultural, continue to view certain species of American wildlife as economically, morally undesirable. While much of the activity of the Division of Wildlife Services involves killing predators ("control" is the euphemism used by officials of this agency) some of the agents are concerned with nonpredatory species. One, against whom the Division has waged a long-term campaign, is the prairie dog. The division "controls" prairie dogs because some western ranchers claim this rodent ruins grasslands by his burrowing and feeding activities. Other ranchers and a good many range-management

184

experts believe that the prairie dog does little damage and may in fact, by aerating the soil, improve grasslands. Whatever the effect of these rodents, the Division of Wildlife Services has traditionally been on the side of those who believe that wildlife problems are best solved by exterminating animals which *may* cause the problems. In this case, the agency has spent a good bit of time and money, spread a lot of poison, to control western prairie dogs. In the winter of 1965, the Division began making plans to launch a sizable prairie-dog poisoning campaign in south and central South Dakota. This is the same area where black-footed ferrets had been most frequently reported and was thought to be the center of this rare predator's habitat.

Alarmed, enraged biologists and conservationists began to bombard the Fish and Wildlife Service, the Department of the Interior with protests. It was argued that the last ferrets might well be killed directly by the poison, by eating poisoned prairie dogs, or indirectly by the extermination of their principal prey. As a result of the controversy, Stewart Udall, then Secretary of the Interior, issued an order prohibiting poisoning operations in the area until something definite could be learned about the status and habits of the ferret. The biologist given the job of becoming a ferret expert was Don Fortenbury.

Few field naturalists have had such a challenging and difficult job as Fortenbury. Perhaps none has ever had one of such critical responsibility, in a sense the responsibility for the survival of an entire species. In the most obvious way, Fortenbury's job was difficult because there was so little for him to begin working with, so few ferrets, no previous studies. Often, while there may not be much formal natural-history literature about an animal, an investigator can go into the field and learn a good bit informally from amateur naturalists, hunters, trappers, farmers. But again because of its rarity, there is not even much in the way of what might be called ferret gossip. When he first was assigned to South Dakota, Fortenbury made a point of publicizing his activities as a means of advertising for ferret information. He did receive a few letters, calls, visits, but they did not produce much solid information. More often than not the supposed ferrets reported turned out to be mink, weasels, and, in one instance, a Siamese cat.

Because the ferret was assumed to be in a precarious survival position, Fortenbury was denied the use of many of the techniques customarily employed for gathering information about animals. For example, upon hearing that a ferret had been seen in a certain locality, Fortenbury could not, as he might have if he had been studying raccoons, verify the report by trapping the animal. If the information were true and he did succeed in trapping a ferret, he might have exterminated one of the last specimens in existence. Nor did Fortenbury dare risk live trapping to obtain animals for study in captivity, or to mark and release them so that they might be identified in the field. Again the risks of tampering with such a rare animal were too great.

A fundamental problem for the biologist was that, in addition to being rare, the ferret is exceedingly secretive, few animals being so difficult to catch even a glimpse of, much less study closely. The ferret seems to be largely nocturnal and appears to spend many of its active hours hunting, exploring, resting, raising a family underground. Under these circumstances even such an apparently simple fact as the relationship between the ferret and the prairie dog is difficult to document. "I've seen a ferret with a dead prairie dog. I've seen her drag it down a hole," said Fortenbury, "but I've yet to see her eat one or actually kill it. I'd be surprised if they didn't

prey on dogs, but I don't know it." The remark illustrates both the difficulty of becoming a ferret expert and the discipline of serious field study where even the most logical assumptions remain just that, assumptions, until they can be verified by observation.

Finding and reading signs that animals leave behind is another good way to learn something about their distribution and habits. However, here again Fortenbury ran into trouble. Ferrets do not leave as many visible signs as do less subterranean creatures. Also the area they inhabit is not good sign country. The plains are dry, baked hard by the sun in the summer, frozen, but with spotty snow cover, in the winter. Fortenbury has also worried about misreading the signs he did find. Where water is to be found in the area—small streams, stock ponds—mink are not uncommon, and occasionally they will wander into prairie-dog towns to prey on these rodents. Considering that the mink and ferret are closely related, of similar size and gait, there is a good possibility of confusing the signs of the two animals, particularly when the only sign is a smudged half-obliterated print left on the hard ground. There is one sign which Fortenbury has discovered and believes to be dependable evidence that the animals were active in an area—shallow grooves on the sides of the little hummocks of earth thrown up outside a prairie-dog tunnel. These are apparently small slides (sliding being something of a family habit with the Mustelidae) made by ferrets.

Based on the few signs available, the best of the reports he received, and what might be called a naturalist's instinct, Fortenbury developed a method for locating and studying ferrets that depended more upon patience—as most field techniques ultimately do—than elaborate equipment. In the late afternoon, Don would drive out into the plains and park in an area—usually a prairie-dog town—where he had reason to think or hope there might be a ferret. He would take a thermos of coffee, a sandwich, and sit in the dog town until the next dawn. Every five minutes or so he would flick on the spotlight mounted on top of his jeep and slowly rotate the light, sweeping the dark plain. Occasionally, one night out of many, the light would pick up a flash of green eye, or a quick movement, and another ferret was located.

On the nights I accompanied him, we went up on a small dog town in the lee of a sharp harsh butte. Don had picked the spot because both a nearby rancher and a Wildlife Services agent had reported seeing a ferret there. Additionally, there were several of the "slide" signs in the town. Finally there was a pressing, practical reason for trying to find a ferret in that particular place. The Wildlife Services agent who had reported seeing the animal had been looking over the area preparatory to putting out prairie-dog poison. Neither he nor the rancher had anything against ferrets, but both were eager to get rid of the rodents and would start trying to do so unless there was some evidence that a ferret did in fact inhabit the town.

Though it is inactive work, there are worse ways to spend a night than ferret watching. A rookie, of course, expects during the first hour or so that each swing of the light will reveal one of the rare creatures. Then you settle back, more or less convinced that there is no such beast as a black-footed ferret, and become interested in what you do catch in the light—lots of big pale jackrabbits, occasionally a porcupine, coyote or stray steer. However, the main attraction and occupation was conversation, both for Don, who normally spent the nights alone, and for me, since the long watch gave me a chance to ask ferret questions of the one man who had more ferret answers than anyone else.

At that time, a little less than a year after he had begun his study, Don had definitely located a dozen ferrets, all of them in South Dakota, though he had one report he considered reliable of a North Dakota ferret. He had had only one opportunity to study ferrets closely over any period of time. That had occurred the summer before when he and a student assistant had located a mother and two young animals living in a dog town on land owned by a cooperative rancher. The ferret family had been kept under surveillance for about six weeks. During the summer months the family remained together in the dog town, but early in the fall all three animals disappeared, whether together or separately, and for what reason, was not known.

Though most of the ferret sighting had been made in or around prairie-dog towns, some evidence had turned up suggesting the association between these two animals was not as absolute as had previously been assumed. Fortenbury had a report from one rancher, whom he considered responsible, that a ferret had lived in and around his barn for several years, apparently hunting rats and mice. A ferret had been killed in a small town nearby after having apparently lived for some time under the board sidewalks of the community. This animal, too, was reported to have preyed on mice and rats. Considering the habits and diets of other, similar mustelids—mink, marten, badgers—it would be surprising, Fortenbury thought, if the ferret did not seek a fairly wide range of prey, in various localities.

One rancher whom Fortenbury interviewed had had a curious ferret experience. He had been riding a horse through the scrub one day and had apparently come close to stepping on either a mother ferret or one of her young. In any event the enraged female had leaped at the horse, bit him on the withers, and hung on until the rancher had freed his boot from the stirrup and kicked the little animal loose. Perhaps the only significance of the story, if true, is that the ferret, like most of the other mustelids, is a hot-tempered, aggressive animal.

As to distribution, considering the difficulties he had had in locating a dozen ferrets in South Dakota, Don Fortenbury was in no position to make an estimate of the possible range of the animal. However, scattered, often unverified records indicate that ferrets may have been found, may still be found as far south as Arizona, New Mexico, Texas; west to the foothills of the Rockies; north perhaps into Canada; and east through Nebraska and Kansas. Roughly this is about the same range as that of the prairie dog and badger, animals with whom the ferrets are often associated. As to numbers, Fortenbury, with good reason, had been impressed with the ferret's secretiveness, but based on nothing more than a hunch, suspected that while the animals were certainly nowhere common, they might be more numerous than had been thought. All of which was just midnight conversation, speculation, not fact.

The mystery of the ferret and man's curiosity is such that a good many students and professional biologists in the Great Plains area have become intrigued with the problem, and in one way or another have encouraged, assisted Fortenbury in his work. Two such men, both game biologists for the state of South Dakota, joined us on the last afternoon I was with Fortenbury. When we went out for our night's watch they came along in their own jeep and parked less than a mile away on another prairie-dog town (or perhaps it was only an extension of the same community we were watching). Every so often during the night, we would hang a walkie-talkie out of the window and check the other outpost. Their night went about as ours did, jackrabbits, coyotes, and no ferret. An hour or so before dawn, the battery on our radio went dead and we lost contact with the other jeep. However, it didn't seem to be a matter of much importance. By that time we were mostly concentrating on keeping awake, thinking about coffee and breakfast. Just as it began to get light, we saw the other jeep coming across the cold, frozen range. The two South Dakota biologists had seen a ferret just before dawn, had tried repeatedly to raise us on the radio. We returned with them, peered at the burrow where they had seen the ferret, but he was gone or asleep. Even so, considering how it is with the blackfooted ferret, there was some satisfaction in having sat all night only a mile away from one of these animals.

Why Bother?

Continuing search and study may eventually disclose that there are more black-footed ferrets in the Great Plains than has been previously thought, perhaps several hundred. However, even if this is the case, it seems very unlikely that this handful of animals will prove to have much impact on the lives of other creatures, especially man. If the last ferret died tomorrow, nobody except perhaps a few ferret students, like Don Fortenbury, would notice any immediate change in the quality of their lives.

That such a thing, the extinction of the ferret, could occur at almost any time is quite possible. The chances are that if it did, some activity of men would be the immediate cause. As has been described, many biologists and conservationists thought planned prairie-dog poisoning operations in South Dakota might have exterminated this species. It was the possibility that this prediction might prove true that caused the Secretary of the Interior to call off the poisoning program. Because of the ferret, not a few ranchers, agents of the Division of Wildlife Services, were restrained from doing something they wanted to do, thought was in their own best interests to do. Whether they were correct or not is beside the point. The point is that for a handful of economically, ecologically insignificant predators a number of men altered their behavior.

Because he is so rare, restraint and negative action alone may not be enough to save the ferret. If we want him, we will have to take positive, constructive steps to have him. This was the assumption underlying the federal government's decision to assign Don Fortenbury to his ferret job. Before the study is concluded, other biologists, other public and private agencies will undoubtedly become involved. So far as the future is concerned there is already some talk and planning about setting up a public preserve where the animal can be protected and studied. All of this—employing and equipping biologists, setting aside sanctuaries, restraining ourselves and others from doing things which seem to threaten the ferret —costs money, time, and energy, not much in comparison with some other public activities, but still we must pay something to have ferrets.

Though it is most dramatically illustrated by the very rare ferret, much the same situation holds true with other mustelids and many predators. Without legal restrictions, positive enforcement of these laws, without constructive game management and protective efforts, the sea otter would probably be wiped out within a decade or so. The river otter, badger, marten, fisher, and wolverine might continue to survive for some time in inaccessible areas, but without some positive help from man, considerable human restraint, they will almost assuredly disappear within the continental United States. The weasel, mink, and certainly the skunk are in stronger survival positions, but considering what has happened to other species when man has suddenly altered the environment or directed his attention toward them in a destructive way (say, because of a new style in the fur industry), there is certainly no guarantee that these species are in an impregnable position.

In the long, and in many cases even the fairly short run, it seems clear that if the Mustelidae are to survive in any numbers, or to survive at all in the wild, we men must foot the bill for their existence. All of which brings up a basic question: Why bother?

I sometimes become impatient with fellow conservationists, naturalists, "animal lovers," who go to great lengths to avoid this question, who imply that even to ask it is unwise and wicked. This reluctance to deal with the question suggests that there are no reasonable, practical answers to it. This is a pity. I feel that the question is a serious, legitimate, practical one; that there are good practical reasons for our species being concerned about what happens to other species.

I think that practical answers to this practical question can and should be given only in human terms. That is, I feel that only if it benefits man is there any reason for men to pay (in one way or another) to have ferrets, otters, wolverines, whooping cranes, or other wild species. Though sentimentalists may argue otherwise, there is no evidence that there is any such thing as biological altruism—one species sacrificing basic survival interests for the sake of another species. Furthermore, there is no evidence that such behavior would be desirable. The ultimate concern (rational or instinctive) of all individuals, species, is his or its own survival. The tension generated by various, often competing survival needs is at the heart of the cooperative system that enables life to support life, to be various. If, therefore, protecting the Mustelidae or any other wild species does not serve man's survival interest, then this activity is immediately impractical and in the long run biologically unsound.

The conventional answer to the question of why bother with the ferret, otter, or any predator has been frequently mentioned in this book. It is that the predators help to control the quantity and quality of the prey species. As far as man is concerned, the benefit of predation most often cited is an economic one. Predators help control various insects and rodents, creatures that are economic threats to man. Also, the predators control the quality of game animals, which are a major recreational and economic resource for man.

All of which is quite true. As long as they survive, predators will constructively influence the species on which they prey. However, it is also true, as some conservationists seem reluctant to admit, that the influence of predators has declined considerably on this continent during the past two centuries and will probably continue to decline. The reason is that this has become a man-dominated land. We men have replaced the predators directly, by killing them faster than they can reproduce, and indirectly, by altering the environment so that they cannot operate as efficiently as they once did. We have replaced them and we have assumed many of what might be considered the predatory responsibilities.

For example, prior to the general settlement of the continent by Europeans, wild hunters such as wolves, coyotes, bears, lions, lynx, fishers, and wolverines were important influences on the number and kind of deer that lived in North America. Today the deer herd is almost exclusively managed by man, by game agents who protect deer, often feed the herds, and by sportsmen who prey on the herds. We have created this situation by both intentional and unintentional actions, but whether we have been right or wrong, there is now no turning back. We cannot, as some rather romantically inclined conservationists sometimes suggest, return the responsibility for deer management to the predators. With the exception of the coyote, who is not the most efficient deer hunter, the large carnivores—lions, bears, wolves—are now so scarce that they exert very little pressure on deer. If man were suddenly to abdicate his responsibility for deer, a biological catastrophe would almost certainly occur, one which would be disastrous for the deer herd (and many species influenced by deer) and cause hundreds of millions of dollars of economic loss for man.

The same thing holds true with regard to the smaller predators, such as the Mustelidae. However many black-footed ferrets there are, 25–50–100–200, they could disappear tomorrow, scarcely causing any ecological ripples. The otter, badger, martin, fisher, wolverine are also so reduced in numbers and range within the continental United States as to have only a minimal effect upon other species. The skunk and to a lesser extent the weasels and mink remain numerous enough, sufficiently distributed to exert some practical control upon their prey species. However, the old argument that each skunk eats "X" number of beetles a year and therefore if skunks are eliminated the world will, within "X" years, be buried under a gigantic mound of beetles is no longer, if it ever was, a very compelling one. If we eliminated the skunk, we would simply take over his beetle-controlling work just as we have assumed the predatory responsibilities of so many other species. We might find killing the beetles that skunks previously killed a messy, tedious, expensive chore, but we would get on with the job. In short, man, not the wild hunters, is in charge of the predation department these days in this country. Where they survive in any numbers, predators can serve as useful assistants, but the prime biological reponsibility is no longer theirs.

One of the problems of the new man-dominated system is that

our techniques of predation, of controlling beetles, mice, porcupines, deer, are often crude, dangerous, and wasteful when compared to natural techniques. We have, for example, assigned many
predatory duties to poisoners, with the result that we are making
large chunks of the environment dangerous or absolutely un-
inhabitable for many species, including our own. The experiment
of re-establishing the fisher in an attempt to control the porcupine
by "natural" means, suggests that we might give much more attention to this approach, finding ways of re-establishing the old
system, or a reasonable facsimile thereof, in specific localities. It
is difficult to argue that the predators would, if permitted, immediately and effectively relieve us of our predatory responsibilities. They no longer can do this. However, the possibility that we
may be able to develop desirable new techniques to make use of
the predators in this regard is one practical and economic reason
for preserving them.

There is a related reason for bothering with wild creatures. It
is that we cannot predict when and how a species may be useful
in the future. (You cannot use fishers to control porcupines if the
fisher is extinct.) Because it is obvious that there are a dozen or so
species in the United States now facing immediate extinction, and
many more whose status is anything but secure, many serious
scientists have become concerned about something they call the
genetic pool. The genetic pool might be considered as the sum
total of all the animate characteristics existent. When an animal
becomes extinct, the genes of that species are removed from the
pool, one avenue of evolutionary development is irrevocably
closed.

Nobody argues that extinction is always a bad thing, that it
would be biologically desirable if every form of life that ever

existed continued to exist for all time. The process of evolutionary extinction, like that of predation, is constructive, allows for change, promotes new species. However, what is of concern to many is that, chiefly as a by-product of our man-dominated system, the rate of extinction has sharply increased. In the last century about twenty species of animals have disappeared from this continent (more than were lost in Europe in the last thousand years). We are simply destroying life, drying up the genetic pool more rapidly than it can be replenished by the evolutionary process. This worries scientists because, as has previously been noted, variety serves as a sort of biological safety factor. The more species, genetic combinations there are, the more flexible life is. If you have a thousand species, there are more evolutionary possibilities than if there are only ten species.

As far as man is concerned, in the short term it seems worth doing what we can to ensure the survival of as many species as possible, on the grounds that we never know when and for what these animals may be useful. For example, we cannot predict when a particular species may be valuable for medical, behavioral, or other research purposes. The whole matter of future utility, of preserving as large and varied a genetic pool as possible has been summed up by Dr. Stanley Cain, a prominent scientist who formerly served as an Assistant Secretary of the Interior. "We know so little about how we are dependent upon other species, how and when we may need them," says Dr. Cain, "that it is only prudent that we conserve them."

Another practical answer to the question "why bother?" is the value of wild creatures as sort of a biological barometer, measuring what is happening to the environment. In this regard, Dr. David Johnson, chief of research for the Fish and Wildlife Service, has commented, "If we are creating an environment that is lethal for, say, a cardinal, then we should be warned not so much for the cardinal's sake as our own that bad mistakes are being made someplace."

The Mustelidae and other predators are particularly sensitive instruments for indicating, measuring environmental changes, problems. They are at the head of the food chain; that is, their welfare depends directly upon that of many other, usually smaller, more numerous animals. An otter feeds on fish which feed on smaller fishes, which feed on miscroscopic creatures which feed on aquatic vegetation. If the otter is in trouble at the head of the chain, it is a good indication that the whole aquatic system is in trouble.

Finally, it seems to me that there is one immensely practical, prudent reason for bothering with wildlife. The reason, which has to do with emotional, aesthetic, behavioral matters, is often said to be so intangible as to be impossible to explain or defend. I do not think this is the case. Quite simply, we should bother with wildlife because we humans apparently need animals as we need art, literature, music, social contacts, excitement, recreation. Interest in, curiosity about, being stimulated to speculate by, taking pleasure from, other animals is an age-old characteristic of man—it is our nature. We do not live as well, as pleasurably, humanly, without some association with other creatures as we do with such association.

At the most obvious level, the human need that other animals satisfy has been explained by Dr. Starker Leopold, a famous California zoologist who has served on many national commissions studying the status of American wildlife. "A great many people," says Dr. Leopold, "participate in wildlife-oriented recreation, perhaps twenty-five or thirty million directly. Many more derive pleasure from just knowing that wildlife, that a black-footed ferret, for example, is there. The minority, apparently a very tiny minority, are those who are unable to take pleasure from wildlife."

As far as I am concerned, the need for association with wildlife is not a frivolous, superficial one which only a few of us, vocationally involved with animals, have. I think that many patterns of human behavior indicate that this need is an important, deep, and general one. It has to do, I believe, with our species' continuing search for identity, to know what we are, from whence we came, to speculate about where we are going. We need to feel a kinship with life. A deep, basic sort of biological loneliness affects us if we are deprived of association with other species, other bloods. I think the loneliness caused by isolation from the natural world quite quickly warps our mind and emotions, makes our own survival more difficult and certainly less pleasurable.

My own feeling is that the predatory animals, particularly the mammals, have a special faculty for satisfying this human need. To conclude with the thought that opened this book, the wild hunters have had a peculiar fascination for us. The reasons are obscure, but certainly a good bit of the fascination has to do with the fact of our behavioral kinship. We see in the wild predators ourselves—the hunter.

If this is true, as I believe it to be, it seems there are many practical reasons for being particularly concerned with the status of the Mustelidae family in America. While I personally would be pleased if I could still encounter an occasional mountain lion or wolf on my Pennsylvania mountainside, I can conceive of no practical way in which these larger predators could be re-established and, in fact, no practical reason why they should be. Their

200

day is past, for better or worse. However, it is not impossible that we can conserve, perhaps here and there increase, the numbers and range of the small or medium-sized hunters, chiefly represented in this country by the Mustelidae. None of them are physically dangerous to man, and only in individual cases are they an economic threat. Though they are wild hunters, there is evidence that most of them—the skunk, weasel, mink, otter, badger, even the marten and fisher—if given protection, some environmental help, are able, willing to live in relatively close association with man, either in sanctuary situations or freely, in odd, unused corners of the land.

Perhaps I can best answer the question of why bother with the weasel clan, with predators, with wildlife in general, by giving a final personal illustration. Though I am more often in places where otters might be found than most are, it has now been ten years since I have seen a wild otter. So what? So I have lost something, a desirable experience, sensation, pleasure. I am poorer, lonelier because of my loss. In this same way we will become increasingly poor, lonely, as we become increasingly isolated from other species, other bloods. The situation will be much worse if we come to the point, as many have, where we no longer are able, even briefly, to associate with a squirrel, a skunk, a rabbit. Trying to avoid poverty, loneliness, trying to be richer in experience, sensation, pleasure, is ultimately among the most practical of all activities. That is why we should bother.